REPUTATION
MATTERS

REPUTATION MATTERS

Building blocks to becoming the business
people want to do business with

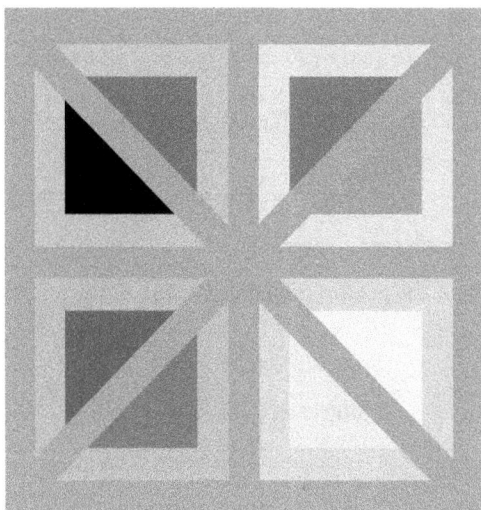

REGINE LE ROUX

Quickfox

Published by Quickfox Publishing

PO Box 12028 Mill Street 8010

Cape Town, South Africa

www.quickfox.co.za | info@quickfox.co.za

Reputation Matters: Turn your Business into a Trusted Brand

ISBN 978 192 0 52642 9

First edition 2015

Edited by Rachel Bey-Miller

Proofread by Delle Jacobson

Cover design by Vanessa Wilson

Typesetting and production by Quickfox Publishing

Available from:

www.reputationmatters.co.za

Amazon & iBookstore

All leading bookstores

For my Mom, who always encourages me to think big!

For Mark Ingle, who keeps me grounded and focused,
and always has my best interests at heart.

ACKNOWLEDGEMENTS

To everyone who has contributed to the book, a very big thank you from the bottom of my heart.

Firstly to my Mom, Annette Le Roux, and my partner, Mark Ingle – a huge thank you for your unfailing support and encouragement in all my endeavours.

The amazing Reputation Matters Team, who are an incredible team to work with.

Also a big thank you to everyone who participated in providing the valuable life lessons referred to in the book: Braam Malherbe, Bryn Morse from Peninsula Beverage Company, Margaret Hirsch and Mothobi Seseli from Argon Asset Management.

The University of Pretoria where the Repudometer® was born, and *Leadership Magazine* for allowing me to use the content of my articles in this book.

TABLE OF CONTENTS

CHAPTER 1

INTRODUCING REPUTATION

"It takes 20 years to build a reputation and five minutes to ruin it. If you think about that, you'll do things differently."

WARREN BUFFETT

Reputations are built over time based on the beliefs and opinions of others. Whether or not they ring true with reality, perceptions are formed on someone else's worldview. Consistently doing things in a certain way, be it exceptionally well or excruciatingly badly, will impact how you are perceived and thus the reputation you build for yourself. The same goes for how organisations conduct their business. This influences how people experience doing business with them and that experience tells them whether organisation resonates with their own values and something that they want to support.

The long and the short of it is that reputation matters, whether you are an individual or a large multinational conglomerate. This book is geared specifically to understanding corporate reputation management and what it takes to foster it.

Essentially reputation management evolved from corporate communication, which the *Financial Times*[1] describes as a management function or department, similar to marketing, finance, information technology (IT), or operations. It is dedicated to sending information to key stakeholders, the execution of corporate strategy through communication, and the development of messages for a variety of purposes, internally and externally to the organisation. It also serves as the conscience of the organisation. This is very often also referred to as public relations (PR), which is described by the Public Relations Institute of Southern Africa (PRISA)[2] as the management, through communication, of perceptions and strategic relationships between an organisation and its internal and external stakeholders – clearly very similar to the corporate communication definition.

However, corporate communication is the preferred term being used more often than PR is. Before evolving to corporate communication, allowing two-way dialogue between the organisation and its stakeholders, PR initially followed a very asymmetrical

---

1   Financial Times Lexicon. http://lexicon.ft.com/Term?term=corporate-communication. Viewed 29/10/2015.

2   *Professional Public Relations Practice and your company.* www.prisa.co.za/about-us/professional-public-relations-and-your-company; Viewed 29/10/2015.

model[3] of communication striving for one-way communication from the organisation to the public, using publicity in almost every possible way. Originally, public relations used in-house journalists to disseminate objective but only favourable information about the organisation. The PR function also used research to develop messages that were most likely to persuade the public to behave in a certain way that the organisation wanted it to. PR is also still often closely associated with promotions, which heralded an era of lavish parties and events to create awareness for an organisation. Hence the terrible nickname of G&T[4] Girls for people working in the PR industry and the perception that PR is all about 'bunnies, boobs and balloons'.

Sadly, for this reason and the manner in which the PR discipline has been, and still is, practised in many organisations, the term PR has, quite ironically but naturally, managed to get itself a negative association. The term 'corporate communication' therefore holds a lot more gravitas than the concept of PR. For the purposes of this book, corporate communication is the preferred term.

Reputation management is more than clever public relations – it is so much more!

How does this all relate to reputation management? Managing a reputation is first and foremost about building relationships with an organisation's key stakeholders. This includes communicating

---

3   Grunig, J.E. 1992. *Excellence in Public Relations*. Lawrence Erlbaum Associates: New Jersey.

4   Gin and tonic

with employees, engaging with clients, reacting to investor concerns, collaborating with government and partnering with the media – as well as everything in between. It is ultimately driven by communication, but it is more than just clever internal and external communication management. It is about looking at the organisation holistically. Reputation management is not a function or the responsibility of one department, but something that is built and impacted by the actions of the entire organisation and all the functions within it.

It is important for organisations to realise that different stakeholders make different assessments, and not all stakeholders share the same view of what your business' reputation is. The personal experiences, perceptions and expectations intrinsic in relationship building are what complicate the reputation management process.

The values of these groups differ and change over time – what was important yesterday may not necessarily mean as much today, and can even have no significance for some stakeholders. It is therefore important to keep your finger on the pulse of what aspect of the business is important to which stakeholder group, and to make sure that your actions and communications are geared to addressing these needs.

Research is key, especially in an increasingly turbulent economic environment and the ever-changing perceptions of key stakeholders. Research also necessitates that the business takes note and is open to the opinions of their internal and external stakeholders.

This book focuses on the key building blocks that influence a reputation. It is important to note that there is an overlap among these dimensions – they are not mutually exclusive. The whole organisation needs to work in unison. You can't have wonderful marketing, but an inadequately resourced staff complement, nor does it help if you have fantastic workers but don't provide the tools they need to do their work properly. Balance in all spheres of the business is vital when it comes to building a solid foundation for your reputation. Figure 1 illustrates what these building blocks are.

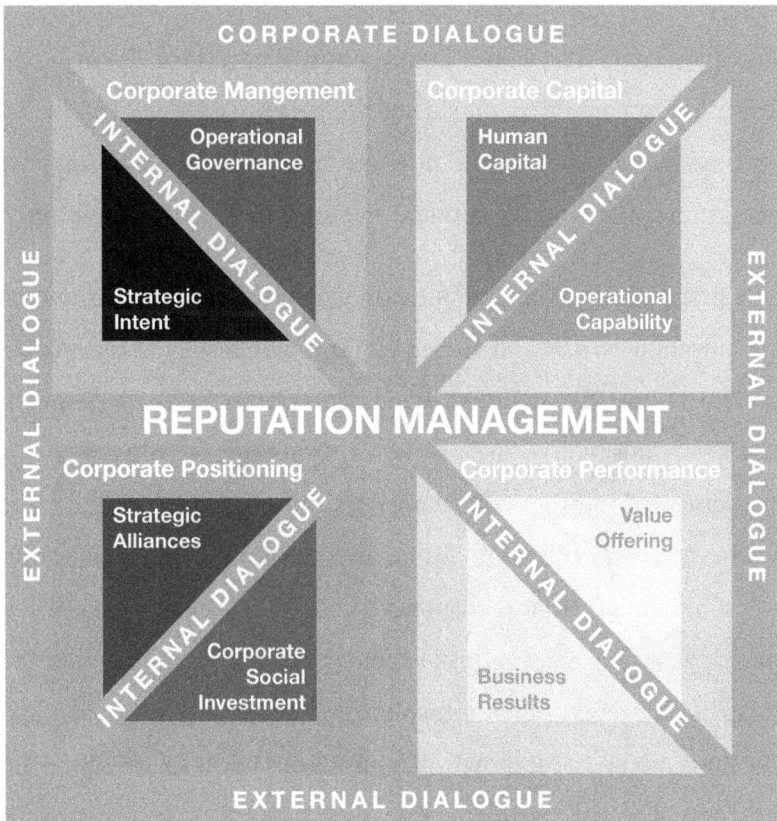

Figure 1 Reputation management building blocks

The key component of building a solid reputation is **dialogue between stakeholders** – this is the glue that keeps all the dimensions together, and contributes to how the organisation is experienced by its various stakeholders. The reality in which the business conducts itself and is seen by external stakeholders starts from within the organisation. In other words, the employees who are the internal stakeholders play a pivotal role when building an organisation's reputation. The way that they perceive and experience their working environment is interpreted and communicated externally. If this internal experience and resultant dialogue is not managed, and the organisation does not communicate externally with one voice, the stakeholders outside of the organisation will receive an inconsistent and confusing message, which will negatively impact their perception and the resultant reputation of the organisation.

The first port of call is Chapter 2, in which we understand how the organisation is run and managed. This dimension is referred to as **Corporate Management**, which comprises the *Strategic Intent* of the organisation – that is, the organisation's sustainability and implementation of its vision, mission and objectives, as well as its leadership. Very often, the vision and mission of the organisation are something that most corporates know that they need, but when asked what they are, every stakeholder, especially those within the business, has a very different version. If the vision and purpose of the business are not clear, how will your stakeholders know where the business is heading and what exactly it is that they are supporting? This will impact the long-term sustainability of the organisation.

The leadership of the organisation as well as the leaders within the departments are just as important because they represent the core intent and need to lead by example. Unfortunately, too often people are promoted to a leadership position because they are technically very talented in a specific operational area, but the new leadership role requires very different skills with which they don't get equipped. Not everyone is a natural leader.

The other element that forms part of this dimension is *Operational Governance*. This is where the effectiveness of the policies and procedures – the 'how we do things around here' – impacts the ultimate reputation of an organisation. Consistently doing things in a certain way, be it exceptionally well or excruciatingly badly, will impact the trustworthiness of the organisation and thus the reputation you build. In the words of Aristotle, "We are what we repeatedly do. Excellence, then, is not an act, but a habit."

The next dimension, **Corporate Capital**, is discussed in Chapter 3. Here we look at the *Human Capital* and *Operational Capital* within the business. Human capital is about making sure that the right people are employed to do the work. This includes aspects such as skills and training, the cultural mix within the organisation, as well as the quality of the people who are employed. It is all good and well to identify the right people, but it's just as important to know what to do once the person is on board in terms of induction and continuous training and development because this, too, impacts on organisational reputation in the long run.

Operational capital is about making sure that the human capital in the organisation has been invested in, has the right tools to excel at their work, and encourages continuous innovativeness in the skills pool. This dimension includes aspects such as knowledge and information management, corporate benchmarking, business ethics and quality service.

In Chapter 4, **Corporate Positioning** is dissected and emphasises the importance of *Strategic Alliances* and partnerships that the organisation has in the market. These alliances form an integral part in reputation building. If one of the partners' values and ethics come into disrepute, purely by association your company's reputation will also be questioned. It is therefore *very* important to select strategic alliances and partnerships carefully. As George Washington said, "Associate yourself with men of good quality if you esteem your own reputation. It is better be alone than in bad company."

Corporate Social Investment (CSI) is the other element covered in this chapter. CSI is about how the organisation gives back and invests in the community. It is important that these community investment initiatives be sustainable and make a lasting impact on those who are less fortunate – they should not be used just as marketing ploys that help create a culture of dependency.

Corporate Performance is discussed in Chapter 5. This measures the perceptions that stakeholders have of how the organisation is performing both in terms of *Business Results* and the *Value Offering*. Transparency in relaying business results, investor attractiveness, profitability, share prices and commercial viability all play important parts in this dimension of an organisation's business reputation.

The quality of and the value associated with the products and services offered by the business relate to the organisation's value offering. This impacts how much people are willing to invest in a specific product or service, and ultimately impacts and reinforces the value of the organisation and its resultant reputation.

The glue that binds all of these dimensions together is **Corporate Dialogue**, outlined in Chapter 6. Two-way communication with stakeholders is pivotal for any organisation. This means timeously communicating the right message through the most appropriate channels of communication to the various stakeholders. It is also important to have feedback mechanisms in place to ascertain whether the message has been understood; thereby building mutually beneficial relationships.

Internal Communication linked to change management initiatives, employee relations, morale and team dynamics as well as loyalty all contribute to employees' perceptions of the organisation. Employees play a vital role in the reputation of an organisation. Very often this is where the reputation of an organisation starts, as their daily perceptions and interactions are communicated to other stakeholders not necessarily directly associated to the organisation. *External Communication* looks at engagement with stakeholders outside of the organisation, be it through media liaison, marketing, public relations activities or social media engagement. Linked to external communication is stakeholder satisfaction and loyalty. Whatever is communicated both internally and externally, it is important that the overall messages resonate and are consistent with the overall strategic intent of the business.

Balance of all these different elements is important in all spheres of the business. Aligning your communication and actions according to the expectations and needs to those stakeholders who are most important to the sustainability of the business will help your business build a solid foundation and enhance its reputation. The value of research is therefore immense, but the value of regular research is immeasurable.

| CHAPTER 2 |

CORPORATE MANAGEMENT

Corporate Management looks at how the organisation is run and managed. This element comprises two dimensions, namely the *Strategic Intent* of the organisation in terms of the organisation's vision, mission and objectives, and *Operational Governance*, which considers the leadership, management, policies and procedures of the organisation.

STRATEGIC INTENT

> *Vision without action is a daydream.*
> *Action without vision is a nightmare.*
> JAPANESE PROVERB

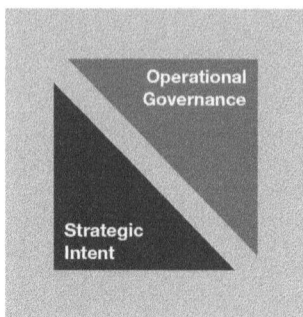

I'm pretty sure your eyes glaze over when you see terms such as vision, mission, strategic goals, objectives, followed by a big yawn and a sigh – these terms get covered *ad nauseam* at management courses, and we tend to switch off because we've heard it all before. The problem is that if we switch off for too long, we lose sight of the bigger picture. Let's face it, we all know that a vision and a mission are important and that we need them because that is what is expected of us in the business world. Without doing a quick search on your website, do you know what your company's vision is? Your answer will give you a pretty good indication of the extent to which your employees and customers know what it is that your business is about and who and what they are supporting.

As much as we are bored with these business terms, they do still play an important role, especially in terms of an organisation's reputation. If you are not too sure about your organisation's vision, in other words where it is heading, the chances that the stakeholders you engage with know what it is, are pretty slim.

Your business' vision is the cornerstone of a firm foundation on which to build a solid reputation for your organisation.

In a nutshell, the vision of an organisation represents a realistic, credible and attractive future state of affairs for a business. It gives direction and indicates where the organisation is going and what it wants to achieve.[1] A mission gives guidance on the purpose of the organisation's existence. When defining the mission, it should not be too narrow, as that would constrict the development of the organisation. The mission statement describes the nature of the organisation's activities, including the essence of the organisation and the nature and scope of the work performed.[2]

Together, all these business terms define the **strategic intent**. But what does it truly mean, and how does it impact an organisation's reputation?

In the end, it is about people wanting to do business with, and work for, companies that resonate with their own values. How can they do this if they don't know what the business is about and ultimately what it is that they are supporting.

Employees play a fundamental role in a business' strategic intent as their work contributes towards achieving the vision. Communication of the business' direction to employees is therefore critical.

Medtronic's chairman, William George[3], explains it quite eloquently, saying that a mission-driven, values-centred organisation is able to motivate employees to create innovative products and

---

1   Steyn, B. and Puth, G. 2000. *Corporate communication Strategy*. Heinemann: Sandown, p. 55.

2   Van der Walt, A., Strydom, J.W., Marx, S. & Jooste, C.J. 1996. *Marketing Management*. 3rd ed. Juta: Pretoria, p. 477.

3   George, W.W. 2001. Medtronic's Chairman William George on how mission-driven companies create long-term shareholder value. *Academy of Management Executive*, 15(4), p. 39.

superior client service that is sustainable over a long period of time. This leads to increased client satisfaction, a competitive advantage that drives high revenue growth, with high profit margins and high rates of growth in profitability. In today's financial markets, these are the conditions necessary for sustainable, long-term increases in shareholder value. This formula is reinforced by reinvesting significant portions of the increased profits in sustaining revenue growth.

We all know this. And in theory, it sounds wonderful. Why then has the concept of strategic intent become stale in South African businesses? One would imagine that it is something that all organisations, regardless of their size, would automatically have in place and communicate throughout the organisation and to all their external stakeholders. It has however surprised me that this is a farce, and that the bigger the business, the bigger the chasm between strategic intent and what is communicated about it to their stakeholders. Very often, the most important thing that is communicated internally is to make more sales, and externally to buy the product or service. The actual intent of what the business stands for, and why people should invest their time and money in it, remains a distant memory of the founding members. Yes, ultimately you are in business to make money, make sales, get people to invest in your products and services, but if they don't know what the core values underpinning the company are, they will be less willing to let go of their limited resources of time or money. Also, having a clear strategic intent will help to identify who should be on the team and whom specifically you want to sell your products or services to. A mistake that many business owners make is trying to reach out to everyone and in the process, touching no one. The strategic intent provides the parameters within which to focus the business.

I have sat at many boardroom tables being asked to help organisations work on, improve and take their reputations to the next level. It is interesting how often solving a reputational issue is thought to be a quick-fix solution. Part of the initial discussion is about the connection between strategic intent and reputation management. We can't do anything with a company's reputation, or know what to communicate to whom, if we don't understand its core business philosophy and values, as dictated by its strategic intent.

On one such occasion, I was called in to consult at a global corporation's Johannesburg office. They realised that they needed to improve their internal structures and communication because there was a disconnect and miscommunication among divisions, which were negatively impacting the local operation's productivity. In addition, the situation had started impacting how they were being seen externally, which directly influenced their reputation and thus negatively impacted their sales.

The topic of vision and mission was brought up as an important link to reputation management. The executives nodded and indicated that they had this 'sussed' and that I did not have to worry too much about it. They had a vision and mission statement that had been communicated to everyone. It had been shared on a folder on some or other network or intranet that everyone could access, as well as being available on the website. I was told too that I should not fuss about it too much, and rather focus on improving channels of communication.

I needed to understand what the employees' state of mind was to determine where to start improving communication. I also needed to identify the disparity between the teams and the overall dissonance within the organisation. So I organised a number of focus groups made up of internal stakeholders on different levels. The respondents were asked a number of questions relating to the basic building blocks of reputation management (Figure 1).

One of the key red flags, which became quite apparent early in the conversation, was that employees were clearly not as 'sussed' as the executives had thought they were about the organisation's strategic intent. In other words, they didn't know where it was heading and what was expected of them. It is all good and well to 'improve the internal communication', but it can't be done when employees don't know what they are working towards.

Invariably, there were two scenarios that played themselves out when discussing the organisation's vision. Either there was deathly silence in which only the crickets could be heard. Or someone would proudly start to recite the vision, only to be interrupted by a colleague announcing that their version of the vision was the global vision not the local one, which had incidentally also recently changed to something else. Another co-worker would then chip in that that version was also recently changed at their team's breakaway session. Chaos and mayhem ensued for a couple of minutes as the colleagues tried to remember and define what the company vision actually was. This then clearly underscored my purpose for being there to start with. During one of the sessions, I was told that they really didn't care about the vision, they were just there to do a job.

The executives were quite flabbergasted and red-faced by their assumptions. They could communicate as much as they wanted to, but nothing would help if the basic building block of communicating the strategic intent to all stakeholder groups was not done a lot more clearly in all the messages from the outset. They also realised that they couldn't expect their employees to perform if they regarded their daily activities as 'just a job' instead of being made to feel part of a bigger purpose they were contributing to.

When internal perceptions are misaligned and a business' employees don't know the vision of the business, how are they supposed to help achieve it?

If there is such confusion about the direction of the company, based on a small sample of colleagues around the boardroom table, just imagine how big this gap is for other stakeholders associated with the organisation. If an organisation can't be aligned internally, you cannot expect external stakeholders such as customers, partners or the media to be on the same page. The wider the discrepancy and misunderstanding of the strategic intent, the greater the impact and threat will be to the organisation's reputation.

Corrective action to bridge this perception gap can be taken by aligning the core concepts of the strategic intent to key communication initiatives. This is done by identifying the key messages that need to be communicated to the various stakeholder audiences and bringing it into all communication activities. Even though there are various audiences, the core of the message should be the same and should be aligned to the overall, single-minded strategic intent of the company. Once these messages have been identified, it is important to regularly communicate them to the identified stakeholder audiences through the most appropriate channels of communication. These channels differ from organisation to organisation, however, very often the most effective channels of communication are not necessarily the most expensive. As part of the communication process, it is also important to have feedback channels in place for stakeholders to give their input, as this enables the organisation to confirm that the messages are being understood, that the initial communication gap is being narrowed, and that the business is heading in the right strategic direction.

Are visions and missions going out of fashion? The terminology may be a bit stale, but the concepts are unlikely to be eliminated any time soon, especially in terms of building, enhancing and improving reputations.

Lessons in Radical Innovation by Wolfgang Grulke with Gus Silber[4], refers to interesting research conducted on middle management's perceptions of how much of their time top management spends on 'strategy and creating the future' versus 'operating the present'.

---

4   Grulke, W. with Silber, G. 2002. *Lessons in Radical Innovation*. Financial Series Prentice-Hall, Essex, p. 266.

How much of their time do you think they ought to be spending on the future? Response: More than 50%.

How much of their time do you think they are spending on the future? Response: 10–30%

Based on an analysis of top management diaries, the amount of time that is actually being spent on the future is less than 10%.

⟫ Things to take into consideration when it comes to strategic intent and your reputation

» Don't underestimate the value of having a clear vision and mission statement in place.

» Clearly define your vision and mission; and communicate this regularly.

» Don't assume that your stakeholders, especially your employees, know what the organisation's vision is.

» Align all your communication initiatives to your organisation's vision so that all stakeholders are on the same page and know what it is that they are working towards and what it is that they are supporting.

» Have two-way communication channels in place so that you can check that the messages you send out are indeed being interpreted correctly.

LEADERSHIP AS A BUILDING BLOCK IN REPUTATION MANAGEMENT

> *"Management is efficiency in climbing the ladder of success; leadership determines whether the ladder is leaning against the right wall."*
>
> STEPHEN R. COVEY

Now that the strategic intent of the business is in place, it is important to take a look at who is at the helm. Who is the person or group of people that is driving the organisation forward?

We have all seen it happen. Monica is an extremely gifted programmer. Her delivery is first class and she gets on very well with her colleagues. Her performance is so good that she gets promoted to manage the division. All of a sudden, Monica just cannot keep things together … things start falling apart … delivery is slow … the team no longer gels … the team is riddled with gossip and Monica feels that she needs to micro manage everyone to get the work done. Sometimes it is just easier to do things herself, in spite of her heavy workload, than it is to trust anyone to delegate to. Monica is on the verge of burnout, and heads a team that is ready to revolt. As brilliant as Monica is on an operational level, she fails miserably as a manager. Monica's spirit and self-confidence are shattered purely because she was not given the right tools and training to take on the responsibilities of being a manager. Just because someone is really good in a specific area in the business, does not automatically make them a good manager or leader.

As a leader, you need to step out of your operational role and strategically see where the department, division, branch or company is heading. You can only do this if there is a clear vision to guide your actions and if you're armed with the right managerial tools and training.

As a business owner, you need to be working *on* the business not *in* the business. Similarly, a manager works on improving and developing the team, processes and business instead of getting too bogged down in operational issues. Make sure that you have the right team on your side to do the work.

A good leader outlines the future state of the business beyond their own tenure, putting building blocks for a sustainable organisation in place for their successors.[5, 6]

In addition to the Chief Executive Officer (CEO), the senior team must communicate the vision throughout the organisation and act decisively and collectively to meet expectations[7]. All the stakeholders must be confident that the top team can pull together and deliver on promises.

---

5   Testa, M.R. 2002. A model for organisation-based 360 degree leadership assessment. *Leadership & Organisation Development Journal*, 23(5):260-268

6   Wilson, R. 2003. Keeping a watch on corporate reputation. *Strategic Communication Management*, 7(1):16-19.

7   Bromley, D. 2002. Comparing corporate reputations: League tables, quotients, benchmarks, or case studies? *Corporate Reputation Review*, 5(1):35-50.

In his book *Excellence in Public Relations*[8], Grunig describes excellent organisations as having leaders who rely on networking and 'management-by-walking-around', as opposed to authoritarian systems. Excellent leaders give people power to minimise power politics. At the same time, excellent leaders provide a vision and direction for the organisation, creating order out of chaos, which empowers people.

Something else that leaders need to remember is that the corporate brands of an organisation are infused with the personal attributes of its leaders. The more senior the executive, the closer the fit between corporate brand and personal brand. The CEO is integral to an organisation's reputation and overall success. In 2002, research showed that the leader's reputation was estimated by influential businesspeople, such as peer CEOs, business executives, financial analysts, business media and government officials, to account for 48% of an organisation's reputation. In 2015, the Global Executives Report[9] showed that 81% of external CEO engagement is now a mandate for building company reputation. In the results, 77% of executives said that a positive CEO reputation attracts new employees and 70% said that it retains employees. Just like any other wealth-creating asset, the leader's reputation therefore needs to be invested in, managed and leveraged over the long term to reap

---

8   Grunig, *loc. cit.*

9   *External CEO Engagement is Now a Mandate for Building Company Reputation*, Weber Shandwick, 2015. http://www.themarketingsite.com/news/39823/external-ceo-engagement-is-now-a-mandate-for-building-company-reputation. Viewed 29/10/2015.

enduring benefits. These benefits include attracting more investors, partners, clients, job applicants and engendering trust in corporate decisions.[10, 11, 12]

Key elements of the leader's reputation are credibility, integrity and high-quality communication with internal audiences about the direction of the organisation. Organisational leaders must, according to Testa[13] and Wilson[14], understand how internal and external stakeholders perceive them if the relationship is to be maximised. The leader must earn the trust of all stakeholders, which is quite a balancing trick, as each stakeholder group has different needs and perceptions, therefore very often, as Lam[15] says, the leaders communicate without making much of an impression.

Either they do not say anything memorable, or they are remembered for all the wrong reasons, such as a bad media quote, poor slides or annoying body language. Worst case: their communication is mistrusted and misinterpreted, achieving exactly the opposite of what they intend. Leadership within an organisation has an influence on corporate reputation, so it is vital to ensure that leaders set the right tone.

---

10 Bromley, *loc. cit.*

11 Lam, K. 2003. Executive branding. *Executive Excellence Provo*, 20(2):13.

12 Grupp, R.W. and Gaines-Ross, L. 2002. Reputation management in the biotechnology industry. *Journal of Commercial Biotechnology*, 9(1):17-26.

13 Testa, *loc. cit.*

14 Wilson, *loc. cit.*

15 *ibid.*

Ettorre[16] advises that intelligent organisations make perception management part of their senior executive training regimen. Consequently, Davis and Dunn[17] and McNaughton[18] note that the organisation's leader has to be the ultimate brand ambassador, and must take responsibility for the brand as the business asset that can define and build real value. It is important to note that this can't be built solely by the leader. Leaders can provide the motivation and the spirit, however, they lack the widespread muscle required to bring the brand to life because their reach into the organisation can only go so far. They have to have the right human and financial support and resources to back up their brand building and to inspire employees.

Therefore, Bromley[19] adds that it is important that the senior management team develop a deeper understanding of brand and ultimately an understanding of reputation and its role within strategy, so that it can be effectively communicated throughout the organisation. They also need to have the ability to execute the business model – this is critical to corporate reputation in most industries.

---

16   Ettorre, B. 1996. The care and feeding of a corporate reputation. *Management Review*, 85(6):39-43.

17   Davis, S.M. and Dunn, M. 2002. *Building the brand driven business – operationalize your brand to drive profitable growth*. United States of America: Jossey-bass – a Wiley Imprint.

18   McNaughton, L. 2003. Sales and Marketing Insights: The Value of the Corporate Brand. *Chemical Market Reporter*, 263(6):13-15.

19   Bromley, *loc. cit.*

That is why quality management is so important to supporting the leaders in their endeavour to execute the strategy and ultimately build the organisation's reputation.

Trust in the executive team is crucial to building a solid reputation. Issues such as misaligned executive compensation and rewards can influence the trust of all stakeholder groups negatively in different ways, and may lead to confusion and cynicism. George[20] notes that in organisations taking steps just to improve short-term shareholder value, the leadership sells its own soul to gain personal advantage; and in abandoning long-held values or its mission, trust is broken and will never be regained. Frequently, it is lost with clients as well and is never recaptured. This is why the process of leadership selection and grooming is so crucial to the long-term health of the organisation. Communicators must recognise that reputations are built through actions, not only words, and encourage CEOs to provide a source of direction for stakeholders.

THE IMPORTANCE OF QUALITY MANAGEMENT

Leaders are the ultimate brand ambassadors. They do, however, need to be supported by their management team to be able to run a successful organisation. Doyle[21] states that the development of a communications strategy for an organisation enables management

---

20   George, *loc. cit.*

21   Doyle, P. 2000. *Value-Based Marketing – Marketing Strategies for Corporate Growth and Shareholder Value.* Great Britain: Alden Press, p. 295.

to build knowledge of and an understanding for its markets and various stakeholders. This enables the organisation to enhance the effectiveness of its core business processes. Powerful brands, marketing expertise and strong relationships with stakeholders enable it to be more effective at launching new products, maintaining client loyalty and running an efficient supply chain. O'Connor[22] notes that, within the context of modern management, it is a prerequisite that CEOs be equally at ease with corporate communications issues as technical accounting details. Successful organisations, according to Schultz and De Chernatony[23], thrive because their management is keen to discover and enact new ideas.

As stated previously, Ettorre[24] mentions that intelligent organisations make perception management part of their senior executive training regime, thus enabling a greater understanding of corporate branding and resultant corporate reputation. De Chernatony[25] explains that with clearer expression of the corporate brand, managers are better equipped to develop the brand. That said, perception management is important, and should be supported by managerial and leadership training courses.

---

22   O'Connor. N. 2001. UK corporate reputation management: The role of public relations planning, research and evaluation in a new framework of organisation reporting. *Journal of Communication Management*, 6(1):54-63.

23   Schultz, M. and De Chernatony, L. 2002. Introduction: The challenges of corporate branding. *Corporate Reputation Review*, 5(2/3):105-112.

24   Ettorre, *op. cit.*, p. 36.

25   De Chernatony, L. 2002. Living the Corporate Brand: Brand Values and Brand Enactment. *Corporate Reputation Review*, 5(2/3):113-130

)) Things to keep to mind

» As a leader you need to step out of your operational role and strategically see where the department, division, branch or company is heading.

» A good leader outlines the future state of the business beyond their own tenure, putting building blocks for a sustainable organisation in place for their successors.

» The CEO and the senior team must communicate the vision throughout the organisation and act decisively and collectively to meet expectations.

» The corporate brand of an organisation is infused with the personal attributes of its leaders – the more senior the executive, the closer the fit between the corporate and personal brands.

» Intelligent organisations make perception management part of their senior executive training regimen.

» Managerial and leadership skills development courses are critical to get leaders and managers to work on the business rather than in the business, and to get their teams to implement the strategy.

OPERATIONAL GOVERNANCE AS A REPUTATIONAL BUILDING BLOCK

You can't build a reputation on what you are going to do.
Henry Ford

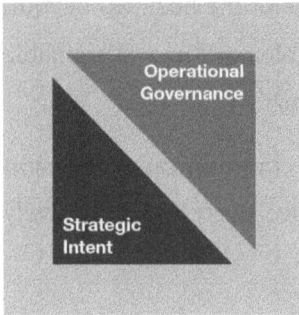

The next key element and building block for a lasting, positive reputation is the organisation's operational governance.

To ensure consistency in everything you do, it is vital that you align operational governance – your company's rules, processes, procedures and policies – to your strategic intent. Things such as how ethical you are and your business practices, also play an important role in how you govern the work that you and your company do.

Operational governance essentially establishes the ground rules for conducting your day-to-day business. It is about agreeing on what needs to be done, how it should be done and by whom. It also clarifies who makes decisions and how they should be made. All this boils down to the nuts and bolts of what the company does, which in turn determines the stakeholder experience. A consistently positive stakeholder experience builds reliability, which builds trust, and ultimately establishes a strong and positive reputation.

In our line of work, we very often see that there is no alignment between the strategic levels of an organisation and their operational levels. They might have every good intention to give excellent service or provide quality products, but don't have the necessary operational governance in place. Sometimes this is because there are no comprehensive policies and procedures, and no clear outline of values, ethics and guiding principles. More often than not, it is simply a lack of effective communication that results in ineffective implementation of the governance structures. It is therefore crucial not only to have procedural structures and policies in place, but also to communicate these internally, so that all parties understand what they should be doing, how they should do it and why it's important. The specific policy, procedure or rule being communicated then needs to be understood and implemented correctly. A two-way conversation will enable feedback from the stakeholders to raise and address any uncertainties before issues arise. In this way, the processes can be refined even further.

Another way to ensure buy-in into operational governance structures is for leadership within the organisation to be seen 'walking the talk', and leading by example. They themselves need to be seen to follow protocol in terms of company rules. They are ultimately the face and 'guiding light' of what is acceptable practice within the organisation.

Similarly, it is important to have operational governance structures in place for all stakeholder groups, including external groups. These could include customers, suppliers, distributors and the media, to name just a few. Every organisation needs to define their own key stakeholder groups, each with its own set of governing structures and communication platforms. It is important that everyone within the organisation is well-versed with company rules for each of the stakeholder groups so that they can speak with the same voice when engaging with any of the stakeholders. When everyone speaks the same 'language', it eliminates confusion and inconsistency and ultimately builds trust in how the company operates.

Again, consistency is key, not only to successfully run the business, but also in building a strong corporate reputation.

So what exactly do I mean when I say that each stakeholder group needs to have their own operational governance structures? Let's take suppliers as an example. Having clear and consistent payment terms and conditions for customer and suppliers from the outset of the relationship, levels the playing field and lets everyone know what the expectations are right from the start. In this way, everyone can plan accordingly.

Another example is the media. Having policies in place on how to deal with media queries will prevent non-spokespersons from engaging directly with the media and prevent embarrassing media moments, especially during a crisis. The last thing you want is the new eager-to-please receptionist giving their version of a story to a journalist during a company crisis. This could obviously cause more damage and chaos than the initial crisis.

By having a clearly defined media policy, which is communicated at all levels, you can be sure that all parties will know what the protocol channels are when a media request comes through – who may or may not interact with the media and what the turnaround times are to provide the necessary feedback. Without procedures in place, you run the risk of being quoted out of context or as giving "no comment", which gives the opportunity for the public to fill the gap with their own assumptions and conclusions, which in itself is then a comment.

Similarly, have a clear vendor interaction process for registering on supplier databases. These clear processes, especially for tenders, are important for transparency purposes and building a solid reputation. Sadly, too often through the lack of transparency during the tendering process and selection of a service provider, the mark is missed because of questionable practices.

BUSINESS ETHICS WITHIN AN ORGANISATION

You are in business to make money and support your lifestyle. Let's say that you have always been a conservationist at heart. You wear your 'green' cap when doing things and support everything that is environmentally friendly. Then unforeseen circumstances impact your cash flow and you desperately need to find more work to keep your company afloat. You are given an opportunity to do a once-in-a-lifetime project for an oil refining company notorious for 'green washing' so that they can get away with exploiting the environment in which they work. Do you take the job so that you can pay salaries at the end of the month, or do you step away and risk having to have some serious conversations with debtors at the end of the month? This is where your moral core and business ethics come into play.

Someone once explained moral fibre to me as the way you act when no one else is around. It is important that your personal and business values are aligned and reflected in all areas of your life.

In Alice Schroeder's, *The Snowball: Warren Buffet and the Business of Life*, reference is made to Peter Kiewit who said, "A reputation is like fine china, expensive to acquire and easily broken." In making ethical decisions, therefore, "If you're not sure if something is right or wrong, consider whether you'd want it reported in the morning paper."

The theory of business ethics classifies it as accepted standards or codes of behaviour and practice. It is a moral perspective that asks an organisation to judge its conduct in terms of what is right and wrong, what is decent, what is good, what is honest and what is honourable. Rotary has a four-way test that is used as the guiding principle in everything that Rotarians say, do and think:

» Is it the truth?

» It is fair to all concerned?

» Will it build goodwill and better friendships?

» Will it be beneficial to all concerned?

These principles have been developed over the years to provide Rotarians across the world with a strong common purpose and direction. They serve as a foundation for our relationships with each other and the actions we take in the world.

Ethical values may be voluntarily adopted, such as a person's belief in protecting the environment or an organisation's commitment to establishing a corporate culture that enshrines social equity as a core belief.

It is said that organisations with an ethical decision-maker are more effective and more productive. As discussed earlier in the chapter, the leader of the organisation needs to lead by example. How can the leader be taken seriously or respected if their moral fibre is questionable? I can't be seen talking about one of our core values being integrity that is non-negotiable, and then engage in questionable business deals. My credibility, authenticity and reputation will be shot. One of my goals is to work towards having a presence in every province in South Africa and then expanding to the rest of Africa. In one of the provinces we were looking at establishing a couple of years back, it was made quite clear to us by the powers that be there, that we would only be considered for projects if they knew what was in it for them. We were blatantly told, in no uncertain terms, that we would only get work if we provided them with a backhander. Needless to say, we do not have a presence in this area.

In Fisher's[26] *Leadership & Organisation Development Journal*, he notes that a particular business can be thought of as taking either a surface or a deep approach to ethics, depending on the leaders' motivation for being concerned about ethics. This approach is then implicitly and explicitly communicated to employees through the conduct of management, policies and procedures, training

---

26 Fisher, J. 2002. Surface and deep approaches to business ethics. *Leadership & Organization Development Journal*, 24(2):96-101.

programmes and the corporate culture, thereby strongly influencing the behaviour of individuals within the organisation. This deep approach seems non-negotiable to me – a surface approach to ethics will not encourage ethical behaviour. That is why ethical behaviour needs to be ingrained at a strategy level and in all the dealings and interactions of the business – it shouldn't be just something that sounds good in a public relations and marketing exercise.

Schreiber[27] wrote a very interesting article about this in the *Journal of Communication Management*, where he focused on the importance of including values of an organisation at the strategy level. This provides the guiding light for all business activities. It is important that ethics, values and integrity are then not just words in public relations or marketing campaigns.

In the writings of Pruzan's *Corporate Reputation Review*[28], he indicates that throughout the world, the media keep a wary eye on corporate behaviour and zoom in sharply on suspected organisational misdeeds. The television news' guillotine and the Internet are ever ready to defame organisational leaders who are accused of unethical behaviour. Don't we just know it! The media will sniff out any and all corporate misdemeanours – after all, scandal and drama are what sell.

---

27 Schreiber, E.S. 2002. Why do many otherwise smart CEOs mismanage the reputation asset of their organisation? *Journal of Communication Management*, 6(3):209-219.

28 Pruzan, P. 2001. Corporate reputation: Image and identity. *Corporate Reputation Review*, 4(1):50-64.

Also, through the media customers are provided with information that enables them to make purchasing choices based not only on traditional parameters, such as price and functionality, but also on matters such as how and where the products and services are produced and what the reputation of the organisation producing them is. People want to do business that is socially and ethically responsible as well as concerned about the environment.

In Fisher's[29] *Leadership & Organisation Development Journal*, Harrison is quoted as distinguishing between two schools of thought on why business ought to be ethical. The first school is that being ethical is good for the bottom line and that ultimately you are in business to make a profit. That said, the organisation must comply with the law and with society's moral values. The second school is a bit more esoteric – business should be ethical because being ethical is the right thing to do.

Being unethical is business suicide and a death knell for your reputation. Your business may no longer be around, but your name will still be associated with unethical practices so it will be very difficult to get others to affiliate with you in the future.

Richardson and Bolesh[30] suggest that reputable organisations protect their corporate images by maintaining high standards of practice, no matter what the circumstances. The most admired organisations use a combination of transparency, strong ethics

29 Fisher, *loc. cit.*
30 Richardson, J. & Bolesh, E. 2002. Towards the See-through Corporation. *Pharmaceutical Executive*, October: 54.

and a commitment to quality products and services to build and maintain their reputations.

ORGANISATION ETHICS INFLUENCING CORPORATE REPUTATION

The words 'integrity' and 'reputation' are feel-good buzz terms that have sadly lost their zeal to overuse. Everyone knows and says that these things are important to them and it sounds great to use them in conversation. However, you need to be doing a lot more than just mouthing these words. If you have to tell someone that you have integrity, are trustworthy and are ethical, chances are that you are not. For example, what images are conjured up when you hear someone say, "Trust me…" Why would you have to tell someone that you are ethical and trustworthy? Surely they should experience this through your behaviour and the interactions they have with you and your business.

In "What's your organisation's reputation worth?", Donlon[31] notes that to gain a good corporate reputation, one must not only have integrity at the top, but also be ruthlessly intolerant of those who undermine the integrity and values of the organisation. When looking after an organisation's reputation, integrity is non-negotiable on all levels. We need to make sure that all the stakeholders we engage with share the same values, principles and ethical fibre.

---

31   Donlon, J.P. 1998. What's your organisation's reputation worth? *Chief Executive (U.S.)*, 50(8):136.

For instance, our recruitment process might seem quite long-winded, but it does help to get the right fit within the team. The same applies to whom we deal with as suppliers, partners, and even clients. Everyone we associate ourselves with impacts how we are seen, which impacts our reputation. As much as we look after and foster the reputation of our clients, we have to be merciless when it comes to protecting our own. If we associate ourselves with people and companies with questionable values, our own values will be brought into disrepute, damaging our reputation. As Warren Buffet famously said, "We can afford to lose money — even a lot of money. But we can't afford to lose reputation — even a shred of reputation."

Donlon goes on to say that communicating the organisation's message to the public and most importantly, repeating the message to employees, is seen as critical. As participants are painfully aware, the price of a good corporate reputation is eternal vigilance. In "Corporate Reputation Management: 'CRM' with a Strategic Twist? *Public Relations Quarterly*, Nakra[32] quotes Pinkham who adds that commitment to ethical practices will help corporations attract and retain star employees, reduce hostility toward the organisation and help employees make critical business decisions.

People who are on the same ethical page have a built-in radar for what is right and what is wrong, and use that to make sensible daily business decisions. This then contributes to a strong reputational

---

32   Nakra, P. 2000. Corporate Reputation Management: 'CRM' with a Strategic Twist? *Public Relations Quarterly*, 45(2):35-42.

foundation. Having a solid, moral building block in place, allows you to then focus on other areas of the business.

However tempting it is in the short run to conceal unpleasant truths, falsehoods lead to distrust in the relationship. My partner Mark Ingle always says, "Tell the truth – you can remember the truth; you never remember a lie."

BROAD-BASED BLACK ECONOMIC EMPOWERMENT INITIATIVES AND THEIR RELATIONSHIP TO REPUTATION MANAGEMENT

In South Africa and as part of corporate governance, which also implies policies and procedures, Broad-Based Black Economic Empowerment (B-BBEE[33]) plays a role in the reputation of an organisation.

Being B-BBEE compliant contributes to building a solid foundation and reputation for an organisation.

It is important that B-BBEE strategies are not just implemented for the sake of being compliant. Rather, the most appropriate candidates should be appointed based on their skill and fit within a company. However, for some corporate organisations being certified as being B-BBEE compliant is seen as a chore, and sadly – albeit considerably less so nowadays – there is still some fronting that takes place in

---

33 Department of Trade and Industry. 2015. *Economic Empowerment.*
    https://www.thedti.gov.za/economic_empowerment/bee.jsp. Viewed 29/10/2015.

organisations to be accredited with higher rankings. It is important that compliancy be implemented ethically and correctly. If not, it could dampen economic efficiency and consequently South Africa's competitiveness, if organisations source goods from second-choice suppliers or promote people into positions they are ill-equipped to deal with, in order to meet B-BEEE targets.

Currently, South African organisations' reputations are affected positively if they are perceived to be B-BEEE compliant. What is encouraging is that large corporates are encouraged to do business with smaller enterprises, which positively impacts the B-BEEE ratings of those corporates and also encourages more entrepreneurship contributing to the economy of South Africa.

⟩⟩ Things to remember about corporate governance

» Corporate governance refers to your company's rules, processes, procedures and policies.

» Operational governance essentially establishes the ground rules for conducting your day-to-day business; it is about agreeing on what needs to be done, how it should be done and by whom.

» A consistently positive stakeholder experience builds reliability, which builds trust and ultimately establishes a strong reputation.

» Whether you are being unfailingly consistent or consistently unpredictable, you are in the process of building a reputation for yourself.

» How ethical you are and what your business practices are play an important role in how you govern the work you do.

» Your personal and business ethics have to be unfailing when running a business – this will have a direct impact on your organisation's reputation.

» The way that you act when no one is around is what makes up your moral fibre. It is important that your personal and business values be aligned and reflected in all areas of your life.

» Every organisation needs to define their own key stakeholder groups, each with its own set of governing structures and communication platforms. When everyone speaks the same language, it eliminates confusion and inconsistency and ultimately builds trust in how the company operates.

» Reputation and integrity are more than just buzzwords to be used in PR and marketing campaigns.

» However tempting it is to conceal unpleasant truths in the short run, falsehoods lead to distrust in the relationship.

» Make sure that you ethically comply with regulations such as B-BBEE.

» The price of a good corporate reputation is eternal vigilance.

| CHAPTER 3 |

CORPORATE CAPITAL

Corporate capital encompasses human capital and operational capability. An organisation's human capital is based on the talent and quality of its employees, and the loyalty they express towards the company. The cultural mix within the organisation, both entrepreneurial and intrapreneurial[1] skills, all form part of this dimension. The operational capability of an organisation refers to the tools and structures employees need to carry out their work efficiently. In other words, it does not help to have an incredibly talented team, if they are not given the necessary tools, training and support to do the work they are supposed to.

---

1   In the context of this book, the term 'intrepreneurial' refers to employees who suggest and implement strategic and creative ideas within the company. It also indicates employees who run specific projects within the company in an entrepreneurial way.

As mentioned at the beginning of the book; all the reputational building blocks are interrelated, so should not be seen in isolation. Corporate capital is very strongly related to internal dialogue, which is discussed in Chapter 6.

Negativity breeds contempt and like attracts like – the same can be said for reputations. An organisation with a positive reputation tends to attract top talent, which in turn contributes to improved service and product delivery. This ultimately contributes to customers wanting to invest their money with that company, which means a positive bottom line at the end of each month.

Ettorre[2] notes that even at the most basic level, employee involvement influences an organisation's reputation, for good or bad. Every employee in the entire organisation is a reputation manager, from the top down. Corporate reputation is rooted in trust and is ethically shaped over time. The character of an organisation is continually fostered by its employees in every external and internal action. It is a reflection of the healthy attitude those employees have towards the organisation. Sobol et al.[3], Balmer and Gray[4], Devine[5]

---

2   Ettorre, *loc. cit.*

3   Sobol, M.G., Farrelly, G.E. and Taper, J.S. 1992. *Shaping the Corporate Image – An analytic guide for executive decision-makers.* Quorum Books: New York, p. 59.

4   Balmer, J.M.T. and Gray, E.R. 1999. Corporate identity and corporate communications: creating a competitive advantage. *Corporate communications: An International Journal,* 4(4):171-177.

5   Devine, I. 2001. Implicit Claims: The Role of Corporate Reputation in Value Creation. *Corporate Reputation Review,* 4(1):42-49.

and Einwiller and Will[6] agree that an organisation's reputation plays a crucial role in attracting talent. What work aspirants are looking for most is a 'great organisation' that has at its core an appealing culture and inspiring values.

Corporate reputation assists in attracting good people and good partners. Attracting skilled and motivated employees enables an organisation to remain competitive, whereas a poor reputation can undermine motivation within the organisation.

Sullivan in Donlon[7] adds that an organisation's reputation is its trust, and this is not only from the client, but the employees as well. Nakra[8] maintains that global strategic leaders must achieve a reputation for trustworthiness among employees through exemplary management practices – empowering and retaining employees, and instilling shared pride. This again links back to the importance of the corporate management dimension discussed in Chapter 2.

With regard to operational capital, it is about investing in the tools and technology, as well as offering career growth and professional development opportunities for the employees. As part of engendering trust and gaining their loyalty, employees want to know that the business has their best interests at heart. It is a two-way street. To get the best from a team, you need to invest in the team.

---

6   Einwiller, S. and Will, M. 2002. *Towards an integrated approach to corporate branding – an empirical study.* MCB University Press, 7(2):100-109.

7   Donlon, *loc. cit.*

8   Nakra, *loc. cit.*

HUMAN CAPITAL

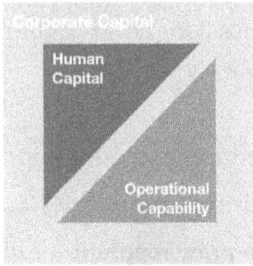

"*If you think it's expensive to hire a professional to do the job, wait until you hire an amateur,*" are wise words from RED ADAIR, an American oil-well fire-fighter who was a notable innovator in the specialised and extremely hazardous occupation of extinguishing and capping blazing, erupting oil well blowouts.

In the previous chapter, we focussed on the impact that strategic intent and operational capability have on corporate reputation. Human capital – investing in the right people to do the job – is another key building block in establishing a solid reputation. Investing in your workforce means you are investing in the quality of your output, the harmony within the workplace and ultimately, your company's reputation. Identifying the right calibre people during the recruitment phase is directly aligned to the strategic intent of the organisation – knowing exactly where you are going with your business and who you need on your team to get there. Getting this right at the onset will save you a lot of time, frustration and money in the future.

At Reputation Matters, we have implemented a rigorous recruitment process. Because we are in the business of managing reputations, we need to be very particular about who we have on our team. The first step is to have really good strategic alliances that can feed into the recruitment funnel. We have a great relationship with the

University of Pretoria's Communication Management department, and offer their top BCom Communication Management honours students internship opportunities. Everyone applying for a position, whether as a senior account manager or an intern, has to go through the same recruitment process, starting with an online application form.

There are a number of reasons for this. Firstly, it shows whether the person is serious about wanting the position – if they are, they complete the form in full. Secondly, it demonstrates their basic use of language, which is vital in business communications and subsequent reputation management. I am amazed by the number of applications we receive where the applicants refer to themselves as 'i'.

The next round involves a phone call to determine how the candidates handle themselves over the phone – if very well, the first face-to-face interview is set up. Should the interview go well, we check references and do personality profiling to get an idea of how they will fit in with the rest of the team. In the final step, the candidate is given a case study to prepare and present to the team. This may seem like overkill, however getting the candidates to self-eliminate themselves has saved an enormous amount of time and ensured that we are able to pick the cream of the crop for various positions. It also allows us to have a continuous pool of talent to source from. Wouldn't you want the best possible candidate to be looking after your reputation?

Margaret Hirsch, dynamic business owner and founder of Hirsch's Home Stores' take on investing in human capital says it is about getting the right people on the bus and the wrong people off the bus in order to have a successful business.

Therefore, once you have selected the ideal candidate, a thorough induction is necessary to help them get to grips with 'how things are done around here'. Margaret takes time out of her hectic schedule to meet and engage with all of their new recruits. I was fortunate enough to sit in on one of these sessions and see Margaret in action. Margaret speaks candidly about the organisation's vision, core values and culture right from the outset, which instils a level of respect and understanding for the organisation and leaves very little room for misinterpretation. It also helps the candidate grasp exactly what the expectations are. This important step links to strategic intent and operational governance, as the message and vision are reinforced right from the top.

It's all good and well to have the right people appointed, however, in order for the organisation to grow, it is equally important to invest in training and development. Peninsula Beverages Company (PenBev), the local bottlers and distributors of Coca-Cola products in the Northern and Western Cape, does this particularly well. PenBev has been nominated and recognised as a Top Employer for a number of years; no mean feat for a regional operation when compared to the large multi-national conglomerates it competes against for this title. What drives their success?

Bryn Morse, Human Resource Director of PenBev, shares that it's a passion for people – those they serve and the people on their teams. He believes that without this passion they would not see the successes they do. He adds that it's about fairness, accountability, continuous improvement and teamwork. By investing in your people – through training and development programmes – you are showing that you value your colleagues and that you believe in their potential to contribute and build a great community and a sustainable organisation.

If you have an employee who is truly passionate about their work, you can be sure that they will be telling their friends and family how much they love their job and the company they work for. This passion and enthusiasm has a positive impact on the rest of the team as well. The same can be said of someone on the team who is not in the right position, and does not share the same keenness for the company. In the long run, both these attitudes will impact how the organisation is seen and directly affect its reputation.

Building a reputation is therefore about getting the right team together from the outset, ensuring that everyone is on the same page regarding the business goals and vision, and then investing in training and development to ensure that individuals, teams and the company are always growing. Another appropriate quote to think about is from David Ogilvy, who once said: "If each of us hires people who are smaller than we are, we shall become a company of dwarfs. But if each of us hires people who are bigger than we are, we shall become a company of giants."

THE IMPORTANCE OF QUALITY EMPLOYEES

Getting quality employees on board is crucial in creating a positive upward spiral when building and maintaining a company's reputation.

The academics[9, 10, 11, 12] agree, employees are one of the most important stakeholder groups for an organisation. Brand certainty and ultimately reputation, influence employee recruitment and retention. Organisations with a strong brand and reputation contribute to lower employee turnover rates.

In De Chernatony's article in *Corporate Reputation Review*[13] he states that employees are not passive participants who absorb management edicts and pass them on to clients. Rather, they interpret messages, become inspired by particular visions and create a brand atmosphere as they work with external stakeholders Again, this echoes the importance of having the strategic intent discussed in Chapter 2 in place. In Goldberg A. I., Cohen, G. & Fiegenbaum's "Reputation building: Small business strategies for successful venture development", *Journal of Small Business Management*[14],

---

9   Davis, S. 2002. Brand Asset Management 2: How businesses can profit from the power of brand. *Journal of Consumer Marketing*, 19(4):351-358.

10   Davis and Dunn, *loc. cit.*

11   De Chernatony, *loc. cit.*

12   McNaughton, *loc. cit.*

13   De Chernatony, *loc. cit.*

14   Goldberg, A. I., Cohen, G. and Fiegenbaum, A. 2003. Reputation building: Small business strategies for successful venture development. *Journal of Small Business Management*, 41(2):168-186.

Gatewood states that management must define reputation-building strategies for attracting competent employees.

Mastal[15] and Anon.[16] note that during the last 20 years, senior managers have recognised more acutely that building and sustaining a favourable corporate reputation helps to create corporate competitive advantage. Organisations now see the part that employees can play in this process more clearly. In this more sophisticated refinement of their roles, employees must project consistent and positive images of the organisation to internal and external stakeholders. Strong internal communications programmes that build understanding and buy-in of the organisation's position are critical in best-practice organisations. Ettorre[17], Post and Griffin in Gotsi and Wilson[18] as well as Kennedy in Harris and De Chernatony[19] agree that at the most basic level, employee involvement influences an organisation's reputation, for good or bad. Successful implementation is made possible through senior leadership attitudes as well as organisational design. Aligning organisational values with employee value contribute to employee satisfaction.

15   Mastal, M.L. 2001. Mirror, mirror. *Oil & Gas Investor*, 21(5):57-59.

16   Anon. 2002. Employee Loyalty: It's Still There, But It's Different Now. *HR Focus*, 79(7):26.

17   Ettorre, *loc. cit.*

18   Gotsi, M. and Wilson, A.M. 2001. Corporate reputation: Seeking a definition. *Corporate Communications*, 6(1):24-30.

19   Harris, F. and De Chernatony, L. 2001. Corporate branding and corporate brand performance. *European Journal of Marketing*, 35(3/4):441-456.

EMPLOYEE SATISFACTION

The happier employees are, in other words, satisfied with their working environment, the more loyal they will be, which contributes to a lower staff turnover.

Locke in Lund[20] states that in general, overall work satisfaction has been defined as a function of the perceived relationship between what employees want from their work and what they perceive it as offering.

Pfeffer in Testa[21] states that the relationship that develops between an organisation and its employees can be the key factor in the organisation's success. Testa notes that the relationship that develops between an organisation and its employees may be an indicator of its relationships with other stakeholders. In other words, when the managers of the business do not truly know how their internal stakeholders feel, they are probably not in touch with external stakeholders such as clients, partners or suppliers either. Leaders are generally in closest proximity to employees compared to other groups of stakeholders. Schlesinger and Heskett in Silvestro[22] and Taina[23] comment that low employee morale may lead

---

20   Lund, D.B. 2003. Organizational culture and job satisfaction. *The Journal of Business and Industrial Marketing*, 18(3):219-236.

21   Testa, *loc. cit.*

22   Silvestro, R. 2002. Dispelling the modern myth: Employee satisfaction and loyalty drive service profitability. *International Journal of Operations & Production Management*, 22(1):33.

23   Taina, R. 2002. Team-building leads to increased productivity, employee satisfaction. *Caribbean Business*, 30(24):22.

to high absenteeism, high labour turnover, a drop in productivity rates, negative attitudes and finally, client dissatisfaction. This is attributable to minimal investment in training, poor rewards and declining levels of client service. A worker who is badmouthing the organisation to anyone who will listen may be a malcontent, but a group of employees who gripe for years broadcast a very different message. They are telling the world their organisation is uncaring, unprofessional, or worse, unethical.

Dilenschneider in Ettorre[24] highlights a central theme of reputation management, namely employee pride. Nakra[25] and Harris and De Chernatony[26] agree that when employee attitudes are favourable, they contribute consciously or unconsciously to enhancing the image and reputation of the organisation among their various stakeholders, including current and potential clients. When employees are happy where they work, they project an equally positive view to the world. This notion goes beyond decent salaries and good working conditions. It has everything to do with sensing that the organisation is fair, open and honest in all internal and external dealings. Even a downsized organisation, for example, can bolster its reputation with its remaining employees by dealing with their anxiety, anger and survivor guilt in an above-board manner.

Organisations interested in maintaining a good reputation take pains to hire the kind of people they want to represent them. By means

---

24   Ettorre, *loc. cit.*
25   Nakra, *loc. cit.*
26   Harris and De Chernatony, *loc. cit.*

of proactive hiring techniques, such as careful and sophisticated interviewing and thorough background checks, organisations can help ensure that those they hire are those they want. They can also include reputation management in the orientation and training of new employees.

Anon.[27] lists factors contributing to employee satisfaction. Trust reflects an employer's confidence in the employee's ability to succeed. Getting the opportunity to do the type of work the employees want to do and having the power to make decisions that affect their own work, are regarded as important. Employees who feel they have some flexibility in when, where, or how they get their work done are more satisfied with their work. It is also important for employees to achieve a reasonable balance between their personal and professional commitments – this gives employees a sense of control over their lives and work.

Our team works in a virtual office and everyone is accountable for their own time and deliverables. Whether you are a night-owl or prefer to get up with the sparrows, as long as the work gets done and, most importantly, the clients are happy, I really don't mind where the team sits and works. A balance between work and private life is also important; I practice what I preach, so avoid working much later than 19:00 at night and also steer away from working over weekends, obviously pending client commitments (and the state of my Inbox!)

---

27   Anon. 2001. What Drives Employee Satisfaction? *Community Banker*, 10(7):42-43

This was definitely not always the case. When I first started Reputation Matters, we had big offices in Sunninghill in Johannesburg with set office hours of 08:00–17:00. What ultimately happened was that I cultivated a team of 'clock-watchers' – come 16:55 everyone was pretty much handbag-packed and ready to call it a day. Work was not completed, which then meant that I worked late into the night to compensate and finish what needed to be done. It was a horrendous vicious circle. I would then be exhausted and take my frustrations out on the team, which did not encourage them to work any harder. This meant that I had to pick up even more slack and work even later to meet our deadlines.

Another aspect that is very important for employees is that they are eager to receive training and counselling to help them excel in their work. By fostering a career mentality through training, employers demonstrate commitment to an employee that could result in employee loyalty.

EMPLOYEE LOYALTY

Pruzan[28] comments that there is increasing evidence that good employees demand more from their place of employment than a competitive wage, professional development and a career path. Bright, dynamic, independent and creative employees want to feel that the corporate values are in reasonable harmony with their

---

28   Pruzan, P. 2001. Corporate reputation: Image and identity. *Corporate Reputation Review*, 4(1):50-64.

personal values, that the organisation provides them with an arena for meaningful work and personal development and that they can be proud of their place of work. These aspirations, directly or indirectly, are related to the corporate reputation. Although it is possible for employees to be proud of the organisation they work for even if it does not receive public recognition, it is far easier to be proud of one's place of work in an organisation that has a fine reputation. Employee pride in the workplace is becoming an increasingly important indicator of effectiveness. The opposite is also true. In organisations where employees are not proud of their employer, there is a lack of trust, confidence, enthusiasm and willingness to offer one's best.

In order to enhance employee loyalty, Reichheld[29] suggests that small teams help provide the necessary focus. Leaders must ensure that team structures facilitate loyalty. The dynamics of small teams bond members to one another. Perks are also good – they can even help an organisation to attract and retain the talent they want most.

However, the source of genuine employee loyalty lies elsewhere. Employee loyalty and client loyalty are closely linked: to reap the benefits of client loyalty, the employees' loyalty must first be earned. Loyalty is not about putting the comfort of employees first; it is about putting their welfare first. In good times, business leaders too often give undue attention to employee comfort, in the belief that employee satisfaction surveys hold the key to loyalty. This confusion

---

29   Reichheld, F.F. 2001. Satisfaction: The False Path to Employee Loyalty. *Harvard Management Update*, 6(10):3-4.

between satisfaction and loyalty constitutes one of the greatest betrayals in the business world. The strongest organisations, it turns out, are those with the most loyal employees and clients, and are the ones in which employees are frequently dissatisfied with the level of service that they are able to give within the structures of the organisation. It is about making sure that employees are 'dissatisfied' with the level of service they are able to provide to clients, and as a result, motivated to reach a higher level of service that they can offer.

Lars[30] notes that satisfied and loyal employees represent value to an organisation, but they also represent security for the results of the future. An organisation's success will therefore depend on its ability to attract and hold onto employees who, in the future, will be among the most competent, productive and motivated employees, that is, employees who are loyal to the organisation and its values, and who develop concurrently with the organisation. It is essential to be able to understand and measure employee satisfaction and loyalty.

Areas that directly drive loyalty are issues that involve the individual person, such as:

» how the daily leader and colleagues interact with and behave towards them;

» to what extent self-development takes place;

---

30 Lars, G. 2001. Using employee satisfaction measurement to improve people management: An adaptation of Kano's quality types. *Total Quality Management*, 12(7):949-957.

» whether they have a positive attitude;

» whether they are committed to their work and are proud of what they do.

Employees want more communication, support and involvement from top management than they are experiencing today. Anon.[31] states that it is necessary to recognise the value of effective, ongoing communication; it must not be treated as an afterthought or an extra. The four most important leadership skills that need to be improved are motivation through own performance; communication of expectations to the individual; treating suggestions and ideas seriously and giving feedback on employees' performance.

May and Kahnweiler[32] notice that many organisations are discovering how flexible work structures, work-family programmes and similar measures can attract and retain desired talent. Such practices are not just 'nice-to–have' benefits but are driven by real organisational needs, such as stemming the talent drain, especially to competitors, and retaining the skills the organisation needs to succeed. There are concrete and visible ways to enhance loyalty if the organisation's culture truly values work-life balance.

Likewise, valuing, propagating and effectively applying intellectual capital may sound lofty, idealistic and useless to a hard-minded CEO. However, when one tears through the fabric of that statement,

31 Anon. 2003. BEE Moves to Centre Stage. *Southern Africa Monitor*, 8(3):1-4.
32 May, G.L. and Kahnweiler, B. 2002. Shareholder value: Is there common ground? *Alexandria*, 56(7):44-52.

what it says is that if an organisation taps into its huge brain trust, the organisation and the people whose brains are tapped will benefit. In most instances, when people are challenged by their work and asked to bring their heads as well as their hands to the task, productivity increases. Heskett, Sasser and Schlesinger in Koys[33] propose that work force capability, satisfaction and loyalty would lead to clients' perceptions of value. That value perception would lead to client satisfaction and loyalty, which would lead to profits and growth. Koys comments that employee attitudes cannot influence organisational effectiveness on their own – employees must also behave appropriately.

Things to take into consideration when investing in human capital

» Have a comprehensive recruitment process in place.

» Have your ear to the ground, listen to what your employees are saying, and keep an eye on what they are doing.

» Build reputation management into the induction process.

» Build a culture of dissatisfaction so that you and your team continually strive for greater improvement.

---

33   Koys, D.J. 2001. The effects of employee satisfaction, organizational citizenship, behavior, and turnover on organizational effectiveness: a unit-level, longitudinal study. *Personnel Psychology*, 54(1):101-113.

OPERATIONAL CAPABILITY

"Technology is nothing. What's important is that you have faith in people, that they're basically good and smart, and if you give them tools, they'll do wonderful things with them."

STEVE JOBS

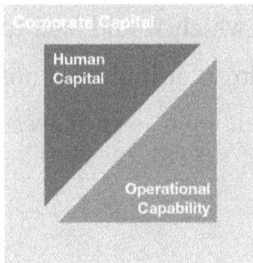

Wolfgang Grulke[34], says that in business, technology is everyone's responsibility. Technology refers to the marketing, investment and managerial processes by which an organisation transforms labour, capital, materials and information into products and services of greater value.

Recently I lost my temper, and it was not just a silent internal scream of frustration, but a guttural bellow from somewhere deep inside me, which thundered down the telephone line. I had been holding for three hours, and got cut off each hour while trying to sort out a fairly simple billing query with a local telecoms operator. After being transferred for the umpteenth time to what I started believing was a fictitious department, not even the funky 'you're-on-hold' music could lift my spirits.

Am I embarrassed about my behaviour? Totally! But the experience just confirmed the important role that technology and a stable

---

34   Grulke, *loc. cit.*

infrastructure play when it comes to running a business and, ultimately, establishing or maintaining your reputation.

Having the right tools at your disposal is key. This telecoms situation reminded me that an organisation's technology does not need to be the latest and greatest investment, but it needs to work properly and be used properly. A chink in one part of your business, regardless of how small or insignificant you may think it is, could have a major impact on how you are perceived and ultimately affect your reputation. You can only be so innovative or creative with limited tools at your disposal – investing in the right tools and infrastructure is therefore really important, especially when your reputation relies on it.

That said, tools don't have to be state-of-the-art. You can do wonders with a single phone line and link to the Internet (when they both work). Mind you, you can also do amazing things armed with a smartphone and the right apps these days.

Taking a step back, you don't need expensive tools to engage with your stakeholders. I've seen companies use their out-of-office functionality very effectively – and I don't mean "I am out of the office and will be back on such and such a date." I mean using it to creatively create awareness of a specific project or initiative they are involved in. One I saw recently was by someone who had entered a marathon and was raising funds for a specific charity – their out-of-office mail encouraged recipients to consider sponsoring them. Although this strategy could be a bit risky, it can work really well if phrased correctly.

In one of our research studies, it was clear that employee morale was quite low, and on further investigation, we saw that each branch felt quite isolated because none of the branches knew what the others were up to. On an individual level, employees said that they felt invisible. With a very limited budget, we tested two ideas. Firstly, we sent an SMS from the Managing Director's office to someone on their birthday, as well as a text to the rest of the organisation to let them know who was celebrating a birthday. We also introduced an internal mailer to share stories across the divisions and branches to keep everyone in the loop. Both these initiatives are still being used successfully today and neither cost an arm and a leg to set up or maintain.

Technology, as Steve Jobs says, is nothing in itself – it is more about arming your troops with the right tools and believing in their skills. Just ask extreme adventurer Braam Malherbe about the importance of having the right tools to conquer the impossible. He and David Grier triumphed when they ran the length of the Great Wall of China in 2006. Myriad considerations went into achieving this world-first accomplishment, one of which was having the right support, infrastructure and the technology of their trusted Garmin and the solar battery pack to get them through the gruelling daily routine. In order to achieve their goal, they had to run a marathon a day, for six days a week for 17 weeks! If ever you get an opportunity to read *The Great Run* by Braam Malherbe, I highly recommend it. It's incredibly motivating and shows that anything is possible if you have the right mental attitude (and technology).

Being innovative and investing in technology also means better use of time and resources. Remember when the Nokia Navigator 9000 was *the* piece of equipment to have in your arsenal? It could even receive faxes! You would never have imagined then that you would be able to do all of that and so much more with a wristwatch in the future. That said, it's important to stay on trend and not to fall for all the latest technology fads, which can be quite an expensive investment financially and a waste of work hours if not managed strategically. Not only that, your dignity and reputation also hang in the balance – a dear lesson reflected in my recent telecoms debacle.

INNOVATION AND INTELLECTUAL PROPERTY

There is clearly a need to build a culture of innovation and to create the need for innovation to happen. Berman and Woods[35] and Tallman and Fladmoe-Lindquist[36] note that in today's knowledge-dominated economy, perception counts. It is not enough for organisations to identify and properly nurture their intellectual property (IP); they must also convey IP strengths to key audiences in the hope of establishing a strong IP brand. Organisations that underestimate the interest and intelligence of investors regarding IP and fail to educate, quantify and communicate, are in for a rude awakening.

---

35 Berman, B. and Woods, J.D. 2002. Positioning IP for shareholder value. *Managing Intellectual Property*, 117:41–47.

36 Tallman, S. and Fladmoe-Lindquist, K. 2002. Internationalization, Globalization, and Capability-Based Strategy. *California Management Review*, 45(1):116-135.

Failure to convey intellectual property strengths – such as number and types of patent assets, strategy, licensing revenue and transactions, competitive IP position and successful enforcement actions – can be a major impediment for organisations that wish to establish or reinforce the way in which their inventions and other innovations are perceived. These organisations run the risk of being misunderstood in the product marketplace, or even worse, being understood too late. If the organisation does not include information about IP in its communications, it is leaving out an important aspect of the investment public's information set.

When being innovative and capitalising on its IP, an organisation is able to strive to be a leader in the marketplace and be used for benchmarking purposes, as being regarded as the most inventive and effective at solving a client need in a specific area, thus laying the foundation for best practices.

CORPORATE BENCHMARKING

Benchmarking is described by Ettorre[37], Adendorff and De Wit[38], Nakra[39], Matthews[40] and Sarkis[41] as a systematic and rigorous

---

37 Ettorre, *op. cit.*, p. 10.

38 Adendorff, S.A. & De Wit, P.W.C. 1997. *Production and Operations Management – A South African Perspective.* 2nd ed. Thomson Publishing: Johannesburg, p. 16.

39 Nakra, *loc. cit.*

40 Matthews, D.H. 2003. Environmental management systems for internal corporate environmental benchmarking. *Benchmarking: An International Journal,* 10(2):95-106.

41 Sarkis, J. 2003. Corporate environmental benchmarking. *Benchmarking: An International Journal,* 10(2):1.

examination of the organisation's product, service or work process-es measured against those of organisations recognised as the best, to produce changes and improvements in the organisation. The aim is to identify best practices with which to identify gaps in the current process. Comparing operations to find leaders and laggers in environmental performance is essential to moving organisations closer to effective practices. The use of performance measurement and benchmarking requires that organisations have hard, factual data to help in setting and achieving goals. This helps organisations identify their own weaknesses and enables them to develop strategies accordingly, which enhances corporate reputation.

Ettorre[42] mentions that the most effective benchmarking is con-tinuous, as the organisation consistently seeks out feasible new areas of benchmarking, eventually integrating benchmarking into strategic planning and corporate vision. Strategic planning is a key application for benchmarking.

Edgett and Snow[43] raise the concern that the success of new services cannot always be measured in the same way as tangible product success. Such traditional quantitative guideposts as profitability often present only part of the success equation for new services. Many other factors, such as cross-sales, client loyalty and perceived quality, are also factors in a success formula.

---

42   Ettorre, *loc. cit.*

43   Edgett, S. and Snow, K. 1997. Benchmarking measures of customer satisfaction, quality and performance for new financial service products. *Journal of Product and Brand Management*, 6(4):250-259.

》》 Things to consider when investing in tools to do the job

» Keep it simple – you can do amazing things with inexpensive technology ideas.

» Align your business' technology needs to your overall business strategy.

» Let your technology choices be kind to the environment.

» Don't fall for the latest fads.

» Consider your technology partners carefully.

» Continuously look for ways to improve your project and/or service offering.

» Nurture your IP and let your audiences know about it.

» Be inventive and effective at solving client problems – this will lay a foundation for best practice.

| CHAPTER 4 |

CORPORATE POSITIONING

This chapter explores how an organisation's corporate positioning – the environment in which it operates and who it chooses to associate itself with – impacts its reputation. This building block consists of two dimensions, namely the **strategic alliances** that the organisation has within the market – the company it keeps – and its social conscience as indicated by the **corporate social investment** initiatives it is involved with.

STRATEGIC ALLIANCES

SUN TZU, in *The Art of War* says,
"If you do not seek out allies and helpers, then you will be isolated and weak." That said, keep in mind what George Washington said, "Associate yourself with men of good quality if you esteem your own reputation. It is better be alone than in bad company."

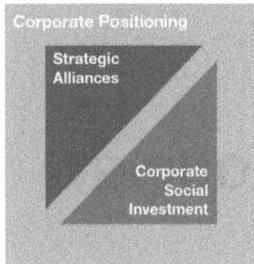

You need to stay true to your values, your brand and yourself when deciding who to align yourself with, be it the employees you bring on board, the customers you want to engage with or even the suppliers that you want to support. All the stakeholders you and your company associate with need to resonate with your own core values. Misalignment of relationships in any way can have a very detrimental effect on your organisation's reputation.

This is especially important when you look at sponsoring initiatives, or finding sponsors for your projects. For example, if you are involved in a project involving learners, then you need to consider whom you partner with very carefully. An alcoholic product partnership may not be the best option, regardless of their good intentions. You need to ask yourself, what message is being sent to all the audiences? Being a sponsor means that the institution or individual becomes an extension of your brand, a brand ambassador. Just look how quickly brands withdraw their sponsorship from sportsmen when they are involved in questionable activities. This is understandable – if they continued their sponsorship, they would be saying that they support the dubious behaviour.

There are six rules or key life lessons that I abide by when making business decisions and looking after our own reputation. They are all based on my own personal experience:

1. Always pay SARS (the tax man).

2. Maintain an audit trail – you can prove something that has been recorded, but a conversation that is not recorded is very difficult to prove.

3. Work **on** the business not **in** the business.

4. Don't do work at no charge – it's the quickest way to devalue yourself and your services/products.

5. Partner at your own peril.

6. Keep family and friends far away from your business.

The last two are closely related to strategic alliances:

PARTNER AT YOUR OWN PERIL

From my own experience and from all the stories I have heard, the positives unfortunately do not outweigh the negative experiences when forming partnerships in business.

My entrepreneurial path started off with a business partner, and yes, there definitely are benefits to a partnership – sharing costs, someone to soundboard with and having someone to share the ups and downs of starting a business. However, invariably there is always going to be one party who feels that they are contributing more, be it financial, workload, time, resources, ideas, bringing in business, and so on. At some point or another one of the parties is going to feel that the other person is not pulling their weight sufficiently and the resentment starts. Unfortunately, after three years, it was clear that our shared vision and core business values and ethics were not aligned and we had to bow out and go our separate ways.

If, however, you do decide that going the partnership route is the way for you, my advice is that you have a very clear contract in place from the outset, outlining the partner responsibilities in as much detail as possible. It is also important to determine upfront what should happen should the partnership not work out. How will things be wrapped up? What happens to the assets? The employees? The finances? What about sharing profits and debts? What will happen with clients? Don't make the mistake I made thinking, "We'll be different and make it work. We have such a good understanding. We trust each other. We'll prove the world wrong..." You won't. If you can avoid giving any part of your business away, consider joint ventures, outsourcing, or getting consultants on board instead. Keep your 'entrepreneurial baby' to yourself.

I recently read *Crazy is a Compliment: The Power of Zigging When Everyone Else Zags* by Linda Rottenberg[1]. From their extensive experience about entrepreneurs, here is an interesting finding: Three-quarters had launched their business with a partner, and 70% of these

---

1   Rottenberg, L. 2014. *Crazy is a Compliment: The Power of Zigging when Everyone Else Zags*. Penguin, New York.

partners were people close to them – a best friend, a family member, a spouse, an in-law. Things start off swimmingly. "We know each other so well!" the cofounders effuse. "Our skills are complementary!" "We practically finish each other's sentences!" Then trouble brews. Cash problems arise, and cuts need to be made. Or business booms, and one partner wants to expand while the other prefers to stay small. Or it becomes clear that one partner lacks the skills to take the venture to the next level. Yet the founders have no mechanism in place to handle these routine disputes. Familiarity breeds informality. Half the entrepreneurs had one thing in common: They lacked a shareholder agreement among partners.

KEEP FAMILY AND FRIENDS FAR AWAY FROM YOUR BUSINESS

This is another lesson I learnt the hard way through the real-life experience of managing a business. It all sounds great – working with those in your life you have an extra special relationship with – a family member or a really good friend. You have each other's backs and best interests at heart. Your core values are the same – right? Initially, yes.

But it does not work.

Due to this extra special relationship – things get 'extra special' to manage especially when business-specific matters need to be addressed and the family/friend-business line needs to be drawn.

The dynamics change when friendship and business mix. I have personally found it particularly challenging to raise performance issues when working with family and friends. I wanted to be the compassionate, understanding friend, and tended to pussyfoot around issues. But I soon realised that that is not how the world of business operates. Friendship does not pay the bills; but those invoices and salaries still need to be paid at the end of the month. Tough decisions and conversations are needed when friendships and business are on the line.

I like to think that I have a close relationship with the team, however, I am very wary of being overly friendly and to 'friend' them on Facebook. In fact, I steer far away from it; I really don't need to know what the team is up to 24/7. Because of our stringent recruitment process, discussed in Chapter 3, I have a fairly good idea of each person's core values. I have, however, learnt that social media is a great tool to look at during the hiring process because it tells me a lot about the person and what they decide to share on public platforms. Speaking of social media, be careful about what messages you decide to share, like or post, as these also become associated with your brand. If you post something negative or ambiguous, it could have a very detrimental impact on how you are seen and perceived in the market, and will ultimately impact your reputation.

My advice regarding family, friends and business– keep them very far apart, and may they never meet.

This is also from Sun Tzu's *The Art of War*: If you are so nice to them that you cannot employ them, so kind to them that you cannot command them, so casual with them that you cannot establish order, they are like spoiled children, useless (Master Sun). Although this refers to dealing with soldiers, it is equally true for employees.

GETTING YOURSELF STRATEGICALLY ALIGNED

Strategic Intent discussed in Chapter 2 prescribes whom you want to target and do business with. Your target market and strategic alliances help you to refine your sales and marketing initiatives so that you don't waste time chasing after projects that won't result in a win-win scenario. Who you have as clients and business associates impacts your reputation.

Part of this dimension is also to understand the competition in the market so that you know who you are up against. This will help you to refine your tactics to grow your market share.

CLIENT RELATIONSHIPS

It's important to know who your clients are as this impacts how best to engage with them. LePla and Parker[2] state that it creates a single focus and direction that allows organisations to differentiate what their clients' values are. This focussed differentiation turns into

---

2   LePla, F.J. and Parker, L.M. 2002. *Integrated Branding – becoming brand-driven through organisation-wide action.* London: Biddles, p. 5.

higher margins and market share over the long term. If a brand is to succeed in the long term, that brand must drive actions as well as communications – the organisation must buy into the premise that retaining existing clients is one of its highest objectives.

Integrated branding, and ultimately, creating a positive reputation, builds the most important asset any organisation has – its relationship with its clients. The organisation and the client control the reputation mutually, but it is the organisation's responsibility to provide the place and take the actions necessary for the relationship to develop. Client relationships are built in the same way as personal relationships. They need to be worked on, fostered and treasured. It's all about professional relationships – people prefer to do business with people they trust and whose core values resonate with their own.

Relationships built through interactions that reinforce trust and common goals create an emotional and intellectual bond between the client and the brand. People purchase products and engage services from the brands that reflect their views, goals and emotional temperaments. A good relationship is worthwhile because it leads to *long-term* client retention and market share leadership. It is a lot less costly to retain your current clients and sell additional products and services to them, than having to invest in additional marketing tactics to get a new client on board.

Organisations that do not focus on retaining clients find that they must engage in higher levels of marketing and communication activities to replace clients who have defected for whatever reason, such as dissatisfaction with the organisation. An organisation's *raison d'être* is profit, and by dominating the market, the organisation will be less vulnerable to competitors and will be able to maintain leadership with less additional investment.

When it comes to understanding the competition, Doyle[3] remarks that organisations succeed when they meet the wants of clients more effectively than their competitors. The information age has brought a marked rise in client expectations. Buyers have come to expect quality, competitive processes, and better and faster service. Schilling[4] maintains that truly satisfied clients will be the first to recommend one's organisation to family, friends and neighbours. A single dissatisfied client will tell dozens of others about their problems with the organisation. One can rest assured that whenever the organisation's name is mentioned in conversation, a disappointed client will be quick to rant and rave about their negative experiences.

Anderson in Durvasula *et al.*[5] points out that a damaging aspect of inferior service is bad word-of-mouth. Studies show that dissatisfied clients engage in more word-of-mouth than satisfied ones. Davis and Dunn[6] and Peklo[7] affirm that word-of-mouth happens outside

3   Doyle, *op. cit.*, p. 4.
4   Schilling, R. 2003. Customer-Satisfaction Confidential. *American Drycleaner*, 69(12):30-33.
5   Durvasula, S., Lysonski, S. and Mehta, S.C. 2000. Business-to-business marketing service recovery and customer satisfaction issues with ocean shipping lines. *European Journal of Marketing*, 34(3/4):433-452.
6   Davis and Dunn, *loc. cit.*
7   Peklo, D.A. 1995. A corporate identity fable. *Bank Marketing*, 27(3):29-32.

the organisation's horizon and control, but is often a huge part of brand perceptions. Existing clients are the biggest and most legitimate generators of both good and bad word-of-mouth about brand encounters. Many studies have demonstrated that, at least in Western cultures, people are likely to tell a story about a bad brand experience eight times more frequently than one about a positive experience.

When an organisation's clients can explain why it benefits them to use their specific products rather than the competitor's, the organisation will have branded the service well and the client's word-of-mouth will help to build market share.

Let's look at client satisfaction and client loyalty in more detail.

CLIENT SATISFACTION

Durvasula *et al.*[8] assert that an essential ingredient for a successful organisation is to keep the client satisfied on a long-term basis. The key to relationship management is to develop, maintain and enhance the dynamics of a relationship with a client. The end result is likely to be a loyal client. Relationship management requires an organisation to view its transactions with clients over the long term. Strategic competitive advantage cannot be guaranteed only by having a superior service or product.

---

8   Durvasula, *loc. cit.*

Newman[9] asserts that organisation profitability and growth are stimulated mainly by client retention. Retention is a direct result of client satisfaction, and satisfaction is primarily influenced by the value of products and services provided to clients. Client retention leads to repeat purchases, increased scope for relationship building and word-of-mouth recommendation. According to Reichheld and Sasser, in Newman[10], a 5% increase in client retention can increase profitability by between 25% and 85%. In order to keep clients loyal, client satisfaction needs to be measured to understand what clients' needs are and how to build mutually beneficial relationships successfully. Testa[11] claims that by focussing on the client end of the value chain rather than simply on core competencies, organisations are better able to understand and facilitate satisfying a clients' needs.

Douglas[12] states that success in client satisfaction initiatives is not merely obtaining client feedback. Rather, it requires turning that information into relevant action plans, then implementing them and effectively seeing them reflected in improved business results.

As mentioned earlier, all the dimensions that build a reputation are equally important and need to be in balance. When building relationships with clients and maintaining them, the two key

---

9   Newman, K. 2001. Interrogating SERVQUAL: A critical assessment of service quality measurement in a high street retail bank. *The International Journal of Bank Marketing*, 19(3):126-139.

10   *ibid.*

11   Testa, *loc. cit.*

12   Douglas, B. 2003. Customer Satisfaction Customer Satisfaction SUCCESS. *Marketing Management*, 12(2):21-25.

dimensions necessary for client satisfaction initiatives to deliver higher long-term profits are the corporate management (Chapter 2) and corporate dialogue (Chapter 6) building blocks. From the outset, the organisation must know what its strategic intent is. It must have top-management commitment and this commitment must be the driving force behind the initiative. There must also be systems in place to ensure consistency of the delivery of services. In terms of corporate dialogue, external dialogue is particularly important – a well-conceived communication plan must keep clients and employees aware of the initiative's implementation and successes, and must be used continually to build and foster the relationship. The communication initiatives will need to include the value of the offering and why clients should invest in the products and services of the organisation rather than those of the competition.

Schilling[13] mentions that generating genuine client satisfaction is often more of an exercise in psychology than a series of marketing ploys. True leaders in client satisfaction have found subtle ways to remind clients continually of the outstanding service they provide. Periodic communication with clients using a vehicle such as a newsletter, blog or social media not only provides a means of cementing that informal, professional image, but also allows the organisation to create a sense of belonging for their clients, an important aspect in client satisfaction. Do however keep in mind that the channel of communication you want to use will depend on

---

13   Schilling, *loc. cit.*

the demographics of the audience you want to engage. Chapter 6 covers the best ways to communicate with different audiences.

CLIENT LOYALTY

Doyle[14], Reichheld and Sasser in Bowen and Chen[15] and Davis and Dunn[16] state that when clients are highly loyal to a brand, there is minimal consideration of similar brands in the purchasing process. When clients are highly loyal, they request brands by name, recommend brands to their friends and colleagues and are more accepting of new products or services offered by that brand. They refuse substitutes and will wait longer or travel further to get their brand of choice. Loyal clients will continue to pay a premium for that brand. Peklo[17] comments that when clients are so loyal to an organisation's services that they will not change to a competitor's, even if it costs more to use the services, the organisation has found the right formula that will work into the next millennium. It is all about working towards having raving fans on your side.

---

14   Doyle, *op. cit.*, p. 62.
15   Bowen, J.T. and Chen, S. 2001. The relationship between customer loyalty and customer satisfaction. *International Journal of Contemporary Hospitality Management*, 13(5):213-217.
16   Davis and Dunn, *op. cit.*, p. 18.
17   Peklo, *loc. cit.*

As mentioned previously, Durvasula et al.[18] as well as Raj[19] also say that it is known to be more profitable to retain an existing client than it is to acquire a new one. Referral from a loyal client is the most effective tool to gain new business. Fundamental to gaining loyalty is an understanding of the needs and preferences of clients, their buying process and key decision-making criteria.

However, Ross[20] and McEwen and Fleming[21] warn that behavioural measures of loyalty are often misleading because they cannot differentiate between clients with brand allegiance and those with no commitment. The uncommitted may appear to be loyal, but they only remain clients out of habit or because the organisation continues to bribe them. They are susceptible to rewards such as the incentives and discounts competitors may offer to induce them to switch. The quality of the product that users buy, the experience they have buying it, the service they get in both purchase and post-purchase are all significant factors in changing perceptions about the organisation providing these products.

When there is a poor service or product experience, a client's loyalty will be affected. Positive experiences help users to build up an emotional loyalty to the brand. Emotional loyalty is true loyalty.

---

18   Durvasula, *loc. cit.*

19   Raj, V. 2003. Technology can be One Key to Increasing Customer Loyalty. *National Underwriter/Life & Health Financial Services*, 107(10):21-22.

20   Ross, S. 2002. Making the rewards fit the degree of customer loyalty. *New Media Age*, (1):19.

21   McEwen, W.J. and Fleming, J.H. 2003. Customer Satisfaction Doesn't Count. *Gallup Management Journal Online*, (1):1.

When users have a connection to a brand, it is superior in their minds and they prefer dealing with that brand rather than others. Repeat purchase does not equate to client loyalty, although it does help to build it.

Davis[22] comments that clients are more likely to be forgiving if an organisation makes a mistake when the clients have a consistently positive experience with the brand. This links back to what we've been saying throughout; consistency is key when building a reputation. This translates into loyalty over the long term and gives organisations some measure of protection from crises. Needleman[23] notes that in these tough economic times, gaining client loyalty is more important than ever. Many organisations cannot survive without repeat business.

Knowledgeable organisations have adopted a three-pronged approach. The first is to have a product that clients want and need. The second is to have great marketing so clients know that the organisation has what they want. The third, and perhaps most important facet, is being able to care for them after the sale has been made.

)) Things to consider when forging strategic alliances

» Make sure that all the stakeholders you align yourself with have the same core values as you and your organisation.

---

22 Davis, *loc. cit.*

23 Needleman, T. 2003. Customer Satisfaction Is Supreme. *Internet World*, 9(5):6-7.

» Carefully choose sponsors you would like to get on board for a project.

» Choose your partners carefully.

» Do business with family and friends at your own risk.

» Know who you want to do business with.

» Understand the environment in which you operate.

» Build professional friends.

» Retain the clients you have – it is more costly to find new clients.

» Be consistent when building relationships and fostering client relationships.

CORPORATE SOCIAL INVESTMENT

"It's easy to make a buck. It's a lot tougher to make a difference."
TOM BROKAW[24]

Corporate Positioning

Strategic Alliances

Corporate Social Investment

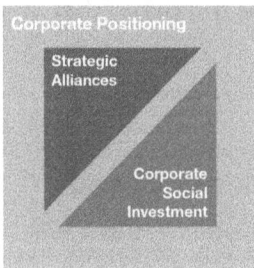

Corporate Social Investment (CSI) and Corporate Social Responsibility (CSR), are very often used interchangeably when referring to social upliftment projects. To a certain degree, they are. However, for the purposes of the research we conduct and the interactions we have with companies,

---

24 American television journalist and author, best known as the anchor and managing editor of NBC Nightly News from 1982 to 2004

we use the term CSI. We have found that even though CSI is not necessarily a new concept, people understand what it is and relate to it better.

The NGO Pulse website[25] gives a great explanation of the differences between the two. CSR is believed to reflect a company's value system and is defined by one of the largest auditing company's in South Africa as "the manner in which a company manages its business processes to generate stakeholder value while having a positive impact on the community and minimising any adverse impact on the environment". This definition indicates that CSR is a deeper approach, as it enhances the morale of employees and the immediate situation of a company's surrounding communities.

The CSR model, which was introduced in the 1960s, focuses on doing good rather than improving profit and other economic goals, as documented by Halal[26]. Zairi[27], Frankental[28], O'Connor[29] and Joyner *et al.*[30] note that CSR is the contribution that an organisation makes to the larger society within which it operates. Many regard

---

25   Ann Bown, *Comparing Apples and Oranges?* Charisma Communications. http://www. ngopulse.org/article/csi-or-csr-are-you-learning-npo. Viewed 29/10/2015.

26   Halal, W.E. 2000. Corporate community: A theory of the firm uniting profitability and responsibility. *Strategy & Leadership*, 28(2):10-16.

27   Zairi, M. 2000. Social responsibility and impact on society. *The TQM Magazine*, 12(3):172-178.

28   Frankental, P. 2001. Corporate social responsibility – a PR invention? *An International Journal*, 6(1):18-23.

29   O'Connor, *loc. cit.*

30   Joyner, B.E., Payne, D. & Raiborn, C.A. 2002. Building Values, Business Ethics and Corporate Social Responsibility Into the Developing Organization. *Journal of Developmental Entrepreneurship*, 7(1):113–131.

it as equally important as the profits the organisation makes. Moir[31] and Wood in Zyglidopoulos[32] remark that organisations can only contribute fully to a society if they are efficient, profitable and socially responsible. There are six key responsibilities to be managed in CSR, namely clients, employees, organisational partners, the environment, communities and investors. Therefore Weldon[33] implies that communication plays an integral part in making CSR happen.

Kowalczyk and Pawlish[34], Maignan and Ralston[35] and Smith[36] as well as Schiebel and Pöchtrager[37] add that many organisations are choosing to make an explicit commitment to CSR in their mission, vision and values statements. Such statements frequently extend beyond profit maximisation to include an acknowledgement of an organisation's responsibilities to a broad range of stakeholders, including employees, clients, communities and the environment.

---

31   Moir, L. 2001. What do we mean by corporate social responsibility? *Corporate Governance*, 1(2):16-22.

32   Zyglidopoulos, S.C. 2001. The impact of accidents on firms' reputation for social performance. *Business and Society*, 40(4):416-441.

33   Weldon, S. 2003. Communicating corporate social responsibility at Go-Ahead. *Strategic Communication Management*, 7(30):4.

34   Kowalczyk and Pawlish, *loc. cit.*, p. 162.

35   Maignan, I. and Ralston, D.A. 2002. Corporate Social Responsibility in Europe and the U.S. Insights from Businesses' Self-presentations. *Journal of International Business Studies*, 33(3):497.

36   Smith, K. 2002. ISO Considers Corporate Social Responsibility Standards. *Journal for Quality & Participation*, 25(3):42.

37   Schiebel, W. and Pöchtrager, S. 2003. Corporate ethics as a factor for success – the measurement instrument of the University of Agricultural Sciences (BOKU), Vienna. *Supply Chain Management – An International Journal*, 8(2):116-121.

Wood in Zyglidopoulos[38] adds that an organisation committed to CSR has principles and processes in place to minimise its negative impacts and maximise its positive impacts on selected stakeholder issues. Many organisations are eager to demonstrate their CSR principles and processes in order to convey a positive image of their identity and to gain legitimacy along with support among stakeholders.

Joyner *et al.*[39] maintain that management itself must be personally committed to such values and commitments, and be willing to act accordingly. Managers must be willing to review and assess their own behaviour. Consistency in decision-making is essential to avoid employee cynicism and rejection of the ethics programme. In addition, managers must be accountable for their decisions and ethical obligations. Mayo[40] adds that there is an increasing trend to impose personal liability on organisational leaders as a means of encouraging socially acceptable behaviour.

Wood in Moir[41], Carroll in Joyner *et al.*[42], Costin in Joyner *et al.* and Lantos[43] are all in agreement that organisations practising CSR help to alleviate various social ills within a community or society. Ills such as lack of sufficient funding for educational institutions, inadequate

---

38   Zyglidopoulos, *op. cit.*, p. 5.

39   Joyner *et al.*, *loc. cit.*

40   Mayo, C. 2002. Too many codes, too much box ticking, too little shareholder value? *Corporate Finance*, 215:2.

41   Moir, *loc. cit.*

42   *ibid.*

43   Lantos, G.P. 2002. The ethicality of altruistic corporate social responsibility. *Journal of Consumer Marketing*, 19(3):205-232.

money for the arts, chronic unemployment, urban blight, drug and alcohol problems, and illiteracy, to mention a few. The justification lies in the fact that the modern organisation has been entrusted with massive economic and human resources and has the power to affect many parties beyond the participants in its transactions. Thus, there is an implicit corporate social contract between an organisation and society, in terms of which organisations agree to be good stewards of society's resources. Ethical CSR is sometimes framed as a way to respect stakeholders' rights. Values, ethics and CSR are not mutually exclusive – rather, they are interrelated and are somewhat interdependent. An organisation's ethical responsibility is influenced by the values of society.

CSI, on the other hand, is defined by Institute of Directors (IOC)[44] as "any social development activity that is not undertaken for the purpose of generating business income". This comprises the cash and non-cash items given to people, organisations and communities that are external to the business. So the essence is making profit while doing good.

For the purposes of this book, we will continue referring to CSI in the broader sense of being involved in social upliftment projects, be it through monetary donations or linking in some way to the operational outputs of the organisation – either way, it is working towards being socially conscious.

---

44   IOC Sustainable Development Forum. 2013. *Position Paper 7: Finding Business Value in Social Sustainability*, p. 6.

In Stephen Covey's *The 7 Habits of Highly Effective People*[45], he refers to the late Dr Hans Selye. From his monumental research on stress, he says that a long, healthy and happy life is the result of making contributions to meaningful projects that are personally exciting and contribute to and bless the lives of others. His ethic was, earn thy neighbour's love.

Covey then quotes George Bernard Shaw, "This is the true joy in life, being used for a purpose recognised by yourself as a mighty one. Being a force of nature instead of a feverish, selfish little clod of ailments and grievances, complaining that the world will not devote itself to making you happy. I am of the opinion that my life belongs to the whole community and as long as I live, it is my privilege to do for it what I can. I want to be thoroughly used up when I die, for the harder I work, the more I live. I rejoice in life for its own sake. Life is no brief candle to me. It is a sort of splendid torch which I have got hold of for the moment and I want to make it burn as brightly as possible before handing it on to future generations."

Finally, Eldon Tanner said, "Service is the rent we pay for the privilege of living on this earth." Stephen Covey goes on to say that there are so many ways to serve. Whether or not we belong to a church, service organisation or have a job that provides meaningful service opportunities, not a day goes by that we can't at least serve one other human being by making deposits of unconditional love.

---

45   Stephen R. Covey. 1989. *The 7 Habits of Highly Effective People*. New York: Free Press.

The long and the short of it is that people like to do business with socially responsible people and organisations. That's what the majority of our Repudometer®[46] research feedback has shown us so far. Whether or not a client actively engages in any type of CSI project, we ask their respective stakeholders whether it is important for them to know about the social projects the business is involved with, and more often than not, the response is a resounding yes.

Investing in the community in a socially responsible way is the next building block towards establishing a solid foundation for your reputation. Although many businesses know that it is important in theory, in practice, it is still not very high on their list of priorities. I'm not suggesting that you spend all your free time at the local soup kitchen for the sake of ticking CSI on your checklist. You need to find something that resonates with the core values and business of your organisation.

CSI should not be difficult. You should not need to start something from scratch – there are myriad established projects to get involved with. You can even see how your daily operations could be linked to local community support, through training or entrepreneurial development for example.

---

46 The Repudometer® is Reputation Matters' proprietary research tool developed to scientifically measure an organisation's reputation. Ten dimensions of an organisation are measured to determine what is building or breaking down its reputation. The questionnaire is both qualitative and quantitative and key stakeholders associated with the organisation are asked to provide their feedback. In this way, we can determine which dimensions are important to which stakeholder groups and work with organisations to put strategies in place to take their reputations to the next level.

The snag is that making a sustainable difference is a whole lot trickier, and takes a lot more strategic thinking than randomly donating a couple of bucks to the local community. Think of the maxim, *Give a person a fish and he has food for a day; teach him how to fish and he will have food for a lifetime.*

It does not help anyone if you donate things purely for the sake of giving. While it may quieten your conscience for a bit to give the beggar on the street a couple of Rand, you are in the process of creating a cycle of dependency because he may start feeling entitled to get the handout and not even consider alternative ways to get himself out of the predicament of being dependent upon your open wallet. There is a very good book by Vivienne Schultz and Anneke Buys called *Dependency to Dignity* on the topic of creating sustainable and emotionally intelligent societies[47].

Be careful not to use CSI as a marketing opportunity. I appreciate that publicity is one of the key drivers when investing in projects; how lovely to have your photo in the local paper with a big cheque and many zeros to boot. Do a reality check: CSI projects are not about how wonderful you look next to the cheque. I once heard a journalist refer to these types of photos as 'crotch shots'!

Although I am sure the recipients are very grateful for the donation, the publicity opportunity should be on profiling the specific school, project or NGO so that they can garner more awareness

---

47   Vivienne Schultz and Anneke Buys. 2011. *Dependency to Dignity*. A2B Entrepreneurial
      Movement: Pretoria, South Africa.

for their story, thereby encouraging other businesses to invest in what they do. This can be done very elegantly; instead of sending through a handshake photo with a cheque, rather profile someone or something about the project. Someone's story or a case study is so much more interesting to hear about than how wonderful your money is. With the right media guidance from your communication team, a quote about your support from either you or the recipient can subtly be incorporated into the release, so that you can still get associated with the great work being done, rather than the focus being squarely on your business. It is also key to work in the CSI message where appropriate so that clients know that x amount of the money they invest in your products and services will be used towards a specific upliftment project.

It is understandable that many corporates don't always have the resources to designate a specific department or team to CSI projects. That's where strategic alliances are important. There are many organisations that can help corporates identify and implement their social upliftment projects in a sustainable way. One such organisation is Rotary International.

Rotary's core is about '*service before self*'. It is important to Rotary that the projects that they take on are aligned to the core values of the four-way test[48]. These are the ethics on which Rotary, as the world's largest International service organisation, bases all its work.

---

48 Rotary's four-way test: Of the things we think, say and do, is it the truth? Is it fair to all concerned? Will it build goodwill and better friendships? Will it be beneficial to all concerned?

South Africa's favourite corruption fighter, Public Protector Thuli Madonsela, recently tweeted that if government and businesses based all their decisions and work on the Rotary four-way test, our country would be in a much better space.

It is also important to Rotarians that the partners that they work with know that it's their policy to ensure that 100% of the funds generated are used for the designated beneficiaries. In other words, the funds are used only for the projects that they were allocated to. The volunteer Rotarians in each Rotary Club work very closely with corporate organisations who don't always have the manpower, or in some cases, the community knowledge to designate a department or team to their preferred CSI projects. Rotary is then able to assist businesses to implement their CSI goals by helping with the assessment of possible projects, doing background checks, ensuring sound financial budgeting and community consultation to ensure a well-planned project that is viable and sustainable and makes a meaningful impact. Rotary can also provide project management for each initiative as well as thorough reports after completion. Regular post-project checks are also done to address any maintenance issues. By operating with complete transparency, both parties are able to maintain a firm hand on the projects and their outcomes, ensuring that the funds invested have been wisely managed.

The next element of success in the integrity strategy is therefore the integration of these values into the normal channels of strategic decision-making. Where possible include employees in the decision-making process in terms of identifying which projects to support, as well as including them in activities. I've heard that some companies give their employees a certain number of CSI days during the year that they can use to support upliftment projects of their choice. In other words, these are not leave days, but rather days to be out of the office dedicated to a project that will benefit the community. That said, it is important that the projects have an element of sustainability and do not create greater levels of dependency.

According to Balmer and Gray[49], O'Connor[50] and King in Howarth[51], an organisation that enjoys a reputation for being a proactive corporate citizen is more likely to gain real long-term competitive advantage by building improved operational and process efficiency, focusing on these key issues: protected share liquidity, positive engagement with investors, lenders, insurers and indexers as well as protection against negative external scrutiny. Building up a reservoir of goodwill towards an organisation could also act as a protective buffer to sustain an organisation against threats to and attacks on its reputation in times of crisis. Conversely, by failing to demonstrate behaviour that is perceived to be socially responsible proactively, organisations can jeopardise their reputation.

Wilson[52] asserts that in order to understand corporate reputation, it is necessary to understand CSI. Corporate social responsibility initiatives have become a board-level concern across all markets. People believe that organisations can really make a difference in

49   Balmer and Gray, *loc. cit.*

50   O'Connor, *loc. cit.*

51   Howarth, A. 2002. Get started in corporate social responsibility. *Financial Management* (CIMA), (1):5.

52   Wilson, *loc. cit.*

terms of creating a better society or a more sustainable environment. However, delivering on a commitment to CSI requires a long-term view and the ability to deal with short-term volatility, such as conflict and economic uncertainty, without neglecting the future needs of the organisation.

)) Things to keep in mind when considering CSI initiatives

» Align your social investment projects to your strategic intent.

» See how your daily business operations could link to a community upliftment project.

» Involve your employees in your CSI decisions and projects.

» If there is a media opportunity for the CSI project that you are involved in, make sure that the project is the focus, not your goodwill.

» Use organisations such as Rotary to maximise your CSI budget to make a sustainable difference.

CHAPTER 5

CORPORATE PERFORMANCE

"We can afford to lose money – even a lot of money. But we can't afford to lose reputation – even a shred of reputation."

WARREN BUFFETT

This chapter looks at the organisation's financial performance.

Perceptions and expectations that stakeholders have regarding an organisation's value offering are looked at. In other words, the quality of and the value associated with products and the services offered by the business. How much people are willing to invest in a specific product or service ultimately impacts and reinforces the value of the organisation and bolsters its reputation. As Warren Buffet says, *"Price is what you pay. Value is what you get."*

Business Results are also explored in this chapter, including some financial aspects of an organisation. This includes topics such as transparency in relaying business results, investor attractiveness, profitability, share prices and commercial viability. The chapter does not focus on the technical elements of these financials areas – it does however look at the link between it and your organisation's reputation.

VALUE OF SERVICE OFFERING

"Don't count your check-ins before they cash."

Vanna Bonta

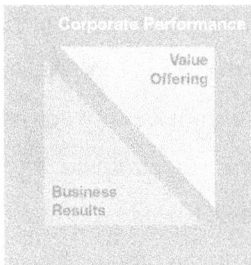

Isn't it frustrating when you have to pay for your parking ticket and you find you are a Rand short and the pay point does not accept card payments? To then track down an ATM to draw money is hugely inconvenient, not to mention the walk of shame when there are people behind you in the queue. It would have been so much better had you planned properly and drawn money when you had the chance. Similarly, your company's finances need to be properly planned. Just like you need cash in your wallet for unforeseen circumstances, so too do you need to make sure that you have sufficient funds in the company bank account to pay your expenses. Cash flow is the lifeblood that sustains any organisation, and a building block that forms part of an organisation's reputation.

Sounds easy, right? Yes, it is. However, surprisingly, it's not always that simple.

To have money in the bank, you need to be paid for your product or service offering, and to be paid, you need to ensure that your offering is seen to be creating value for your stakeholders. You also need to have systems in place to receive payments.

To build your reputation, customers need to recognise the value in what you have to offer, and must want to and be able to spend their hard-earned cash on your offering instead of the competition's. The more highly people regard this value, the more likely they will be to invest in the offering and remain loyal customers in the long run.

It is all a balancing act, and the crux is consistency across the entire business. Yes, gaining customer loyalty is essential – however, when building a reputation it is crucial to maintain quality across all the divisions and business units for all the stakeholders who are associated with the organisation. In other words, suppliers, partners, employees and sponsors should all be treated with the same high regard as customers because they add to the value of the organisation and its offerings.

This is very often where companies get it wrong, and where corporate South Africa falls short. They deliver amazing products and services, and invest in expensive campaigns to set themselves apart from their competition. They are quick off the mark to respond to negative social media posts. However, they forget about their other stakeholders, such as their suppliers, and don't think about the impact that their policies and payment terms have on them. We have all heard and read a lot about corporates wanting to invest in and support SMMEs[1] as this can positively impact their B-BBEE ratings. In theory, this is great but the snag is that more often than not, the payment terms are unrealistic.

We recently worked with a large organisation that I have always held in very high regard because of the service they deliver and the way that they engage with their customers. However, being on the other side of the coin as a service provider has definitely tarnished my view of them. Their 30-day payment terms are a standard agreement that I respect, however our invoice was 'lost' in the system and the 30 days only started on the day they retrieved it. I was told that some companies are still waiting for invoices to be settled from five months ago. This was not as reassuring as they tried to make it sound. It's a vicious circle, which could all have been prevented if proper structures were in place to settle invoices when they are due. Supporting smaller organisations from a thin, insufficient and unsteady cash flow, to well-planned abundance is what I like to call Cash Glow™[2]. This boils down to nurturing and growing your bottom line, which is essential to the stability, growth and prosperity of a business.

---

1   Small, Medium and Micro-sized Enterprises.

2   I have the trademark for this; I registered the term as it is such a fundamental part of a successful business.

To get Cash Glow, it is very important to plan and have processes in place so that everyone knows what is expected from them – where, when and how. It is also important to stick to the agreed terms.

Personally, I dislike having to follow up on payments due, so I've had to find ways to avoid awkward conversations to get our invoices paid on time.

Here are my top ten tips:

» Invest in a really good accountant to help you keep on top of your finances.

» Ideally, get payment before doing the work. A dynamic business owner that I have a high regard for explained it really well: you need to pay for your groceries before you leave the store, you don't pay for the food only once you've eaten it. Why bill for your products and services any differently?

» Create a savings or call account and keep the payments you receive in there and budget only for the expenses you have. Save the rest of the money for larger payments that you know will become due such as VAT – in this way, you won't be tempted to use it for other expenses.

» For invoices that go out on a regular basis, or that don't get paid upfront; send them out early in the month. We want payment by the 25th of the month, so we send out invoices by the 16th. I have heard that some businesses send theirs out even earlier in the month. My experience has been that a week in advance is sufficient for most customers.

» In the past, we only sent the first reminder for invoices the day before payment was due. However, we've started sending out the first reminder three days before the payment date. This includes a reminder to the customer what was delivered, any value added services and the agreed terms.

» If we don't receive payment on the agreed date, the person working on the account then follows up with the customer. Fortunately, this happens very rarely.

» If payment is still not received by the last day of the month, I get involved by making a phone call to the client to follow up on the payment. Again, fortunately, this is rarely necessary.

» That said, interest is charged on overdue payments the next time the invoice goes out. This is communicated and agreed with customers as part of our terms of engagement on commencement of projects. Banks and SARS don't think twice about charging you interest or late payment penalties – why should doing business with corporates be any different? I see no reason why we should carry that cost.

» Sticking to the process is important so that everyone on our side and the clients' side knows what to expect and what to do.

» It is important to acknowledge the payment and to thank the customer once it has been received.

PRODUCTS AND SERVICES

"Start by doing what is necessary, then do what is possible,
and suddenly you are doing the impossible."
St. Francis of Assisi

LePla and Parker[3] explain that when an organisation is brand-driven from the beginning, it is able to leverage all the skills of all workers in a direction that makes best use of their strengths. I'd like to take this a step further, and say that an organisation should be reputation-driven from the beginning, and align the service/product offering to its strategic intent. This process provides immediate strategic direction for product/service development. An organisation should produce products that correspond more exactly to its strengths, builds value, trust and loyalty among clients faster than the competition.

Let's take a closer look at three important aspects of products and services – quality, flexibility and innovation.

QUALITY

According to Grunig[4], total quality is a priority, not only in words or in the organisation's philosophy statement – it is a priority when actions are taken, decisions are made or resources are allocated. The extent to which an organisation pays attention

---

3   LePla and Parker, *op. cit.*, p. 4.
4   Grunig, *loc. cit.*

to quality is a characteristic of excellence provided by the total quality movement[5].

Van der Walt *et al.*[6] note that from a marketing point of view, a product in the broadest sense can be defined as a collection of need-satisfying utilities, offered to a market so that the market can pay attention to it, buy it or consume it. Physical objects, services, personalities, places, institutions and ideas are all products. Lesle and Sheth in Durvasula, Lysonski and Mehta[7] note that over the last decade, service organisations have identified quality as a driving force in the success of their organisations and in developing a sustainable competitive advantage.

Services are different from tangible products, as they are produced and consumed simultaneously and the delivery of the service is often inseparable from the employees who provide it. While it is impossible for service organisations to provide flawless service delivery in every transaction, the way an organisation responds to a client's post-consumption dissatisfaction may have a crucial impact

---

5   Total quality movement practitioners have striven to develop effective management processes that increase organisational efficiency and effectiveness, enhance product quality, and maximise customer satisfaction. However, based upon many researchers, it should be noted that the total quality movement has failed to have a significant and lasting positive impact on organisations (Giroux & Landry, 1998;) Hubiak & O'Donnell, (1996). For more information: http://www.academia.edu/948786/An_Analysis_of_the_ Total_Quality_Movement_In_Search_of_Quality_Enhancement_through_ Structural_and_Strategic_Synthesis

6   Van der Walt *et al.*, *loc. cit.*

7   Durvasula *et al.*, *loc. cit.*

on retaining the client and can lead to positive word-of-mouth and referrals for future business.

Edvardsson in Durvasula *et al.*[8] suggests that if quality service is to be rendered, the following are necessary: the employees must be quality driven, considerate to existing clients, attentive to signs of dissatisfaction among clients and discover quality defects before the client complains. The employees should make complaining easy. Richardson and Bolesh[9] state that reputable organisations protect their corporate images [and reputations] by maintaining high standards of practice no matter the circumstances. The most admired organisations use commitment to quality products and services to build and maintain their reputations.

Goldberg *et al.*[10] comment that public certification of product quality can be sought from accrediting agencies, assistance obtained from prestigious product development funds and prizes won at local and international competitions.

FLEXIBILITY

Haller and Boyd[11] state that segmentation strategies can improve the product market matrix. Rather than appear as a haphazard

8   Durvasula *et al.*, *loc. cit.*

9   Richardson and Bolesh, *loc. cit.*

10   Goldberg *et al.*, *loc. cit.*

11   Haller, T. and Boyd, H. 1981. Fixing the Corporate Image. *Journal of Business Strategy.* 2(1):65-70.

chaser after new product ventures, the organisation that pursues a coherent, calculated programme of segmentation development might create a better image for itself than its less strategically orientated competitors. A positive reputation, possibly based on strong relationships with pre-eminent organisations in the industry, may be crucial for buyers who will become dependent on a particular organisation's product or service.

INNOVATION

There are clear advantages to dynamic exploitation of available assets in the rapidly changing business world, according to Barney in Goldberg *et al.*[12]. A contemporary option, according to the author, is capitalising quickly on new opportunities, allowing an organisation with an imperfect product nevertheless to capture a substantial share of a developing market and to contribute to the visibility and legitimacy of the organisation. In the long term, investors will be pleased with speedy shipments of initial products and an early cash flow, and as a result, they may provide the additional capital necessary for greater financial independence and reinvestment into product development. In contrast, Porter in Goldberg *et al.*[13] emphasises that it would be of greater benefit for an organisation to consider a long-term investment in core competencies to strengthen the organisation's functional activities and develop a unique product based on innovation and quality.

---

12 Goldberg *et al.*, *loc. cit.*

13 *ibid.*

Crawford in Avlonitis and Papastathopoulou[14] believes that establishing a programme for developing new products may be the most profitable growth strategy compared to mergers, acquisitions or joint ventures. In addition, Craig and Hart in Avlonitis and Papastathopoulou[15] declare that innovation is a necessity rather than a strategic option, which is particularly true as organisations face an increasingly turbulent external environment, shorter life cycles, industry maturity and eroding margins, as well as the ever-quickening pace of technological advances.

Davis and Dunn[16] claim that strong brands allow for greater success with new products because of the implied endorsement. Strong brands and their resultant reputation, lend immediate credibility to new product introductions. A brand can further its value by extending to sub-brands and endorsed brands.

However, Booker[17] states that there has always been tension between corporate brand and product marketing proponents, as an economic downturn tends to push organisations toward short-term, tactical choices that maximise revenue. Slashing research and development or business development budgets also belongs in this category. These expenses lose in an equation in which future assets

---

14 Avlonitis, J. and Papastathopoulou, P. 2000. Marketing communications and product performance: innovative vs. non-innovative new retail financial products. *The International Journal of Bank Marketing*, 18(1):27-41.

15 *ibid.*

16 Davis and Dunn, *loc. cit.*

17 Booker, E. 2002. Valuing the corporate brand in a downtown. *B to B*, 87(6):8.

such as 'an innovative product' or 'a familiar brand' are much more difficult to quantify than current assets such as 'sales in the pipeline.'

Goldberg et al.[18] identified the necessity of developing core competencies, according to which management follows a long-term perspective, undertaking significant investments in a build-up of internal capabilities. The organisation constructs a good name through marketing of innovative quality products with high product value and good servicing.

THE VALUE OF OFFERINGS

As stated by Van der Walt et al.[19], price is the only element that produces income. It has the most immediate and direct impact on an organisation's profitability. Organisations need to be sensitive to the price expectations of the specific stakeholders. Factors that influence the price decision of the organisation are clients, the authorities and competitors. Price does not function in isolation. Doyle[20] asserts that it is not enough for an organisation to produce a good product; it also has to communicate its values effectively to potential clients. The organisation has to invest in communication to make people aware of the product, with specific emphasis on the value of what is offered.

---

18   Goldberg et al., loc. cit.
19   Van der Walt et al., loc. cit.
20   Doyle, op. cit., p. 295.

Davis and Dunn[21] concur that there are definite benefits tied to leveraging a brand more effectively, namely that strong brands allow for premium pricing versus competitive products. Strong brands also give an organisation protection against price wars, which leads to a strong corporate reputation. Alsop in Nakra[22] states that product quality, innovation and good value are all keys to a good reputation in an industry.

Considering the value of offerings reminds me of one of the business lessons I shared in Chapter 4 – always charge for your products or service rendered, don't give things away free of charge. After investing extensively of my own time as a favour to help and guide someone with their business' social media over a December holiday, I was barely thanked. In fact, all I did receive was their disappointment that I had not generated immediate new sales and business leads. I realised that you do absolutely no one any favours by doing things for nothing – if anything, you just devalue yourself, and your product or service. This is the quickest way to diminish your value offering.

---

21 Davis and Dunn, *loc. cit.*
22 Nakra, *loc. cit.*

» Things to keep in mind when considering the value of offerings

» Make sure that you have sufficient cash flow and can invest back into product/service development.

» Have a process in place to ensure payment for products and services.

» Have a pricing process in place and communicate the associated value so that you don't undersell yourself, and that clients still see value in your product/service.

» Invest in communicating the value offering and what the benefits and return on investment are, when they select your products or services.

» Invest in research for long-term sustainability.

» Continual innovation is important in addressing client needs and will enhance client belief in your products. If clients are familiar with your organisation and have a high regard for your products and services, they will be more likely to invest in your products and services than those of the competition.

» Steer away from giving your products and service away free of charge. This is the quickest way to diminish their value.

BUSINESS RESULTS

"When you're building a business or joining a company, you have to be transparent; you can't have two sets of information for two sets of people."

HOWARD SCHULTZ, Chairman and CEO of Starbucks.

Most people are quite sensitive and emotional about money and all things financial, and they tend to be tight lipped on the subject. In the business world, transparency and playing open cards are key to financial health, shareholder value and even non-financial reporting, all of which contributes to an organisation's overall reputation. Communicating **business results** is the next building block in the reputation management sphere.

Financial accounting is something that I will unashamedly admit is not my forte in life. I knew very early on in my academic career that accounting would not be one of my majors or my career path of choice. In fact, it may well have been in my first month of studying Accounting 101 that I decided if I were ever to run my own business, I would invest in the services of an accountant. I saw very little point in studying this compulsory subject because, at that time, I had no inclination or desire to start my own business[23]. The need for an accountant's services was the last thing on my mind as I grumbled my way through the Accounting classes.

---

23 Note to self: *Never say never.*

It wasn't until five years after completing my studies that I ventured out to start Reputation Matters. Appreciating my accounting limitations and keeping to what I had said while studying, I engaged the services of a professional accountant. I use the term 'professional' very loosely. Over the years, I have invested in *many* accountants. Two accounting lessons have been learnt – there is no such thing as creative accounting; and it really *is* important to know what is going on in your books. SARS will need to be paid whether you are creative or not, and I have found that the more creative the accountant tries to be, the more colourful your language will be in the long-run.

It took me eight painful years to find the right accountant. It was only when I found good quality accountants that I truly appreciated the importance of transparency, and realised how many businesses there are out there whose ethics are questionable.

A lack of transparency and unethical creativity will undoubtedly cause a dent in any organisation's reputation, which is why integrity should be non-negotiable on all levels, including your own and your suppliers.

The level of transparency about how funds are generated, invested and spent, plays a significant role in an organisation's reputation.

In the global financial marketplace, a favourable reputation is regarded as a prerequisite to success. It's about creating shareholder value. Shareholders can ultimately give or withhold their approval of management through their votes. In addition, their decisions on buying and selling influence share prices. An unfavourable reputation therefore, has a direct and measurable impact on an organisation's share price.

How then, is shareholder value created, built and leveraged? I turned to Argon Asset Management Chief Executive Officer and Co-founder Mothobi Seseli for his thoughts on the subject and to find out what their recipe for success is. I am in awe of what Mothobi and his team have achieved since their the company's inception in 2005. He and his co-founders have been successfully building a black-owned asset management firm that has become a force for good in our country. Argon now manages ZAR 30bn[24] in client assets, and offers listed investment strategies in equities, fixed income and multi asset class, both domestically and globally. It is set to expand into the retail space – no small feat in this extremely competitive environment.

Mothobi shares, "It has been an incredibly challenging journey for Argon to break down traditional barriers to entry. However, through our non-compromising values and ethical standards, we continue to build a strong track record and work really hard to achieve excellence for clients who have confidence in us."

Mothobi continues, "When it comes to creating value, it is all about upholding our values of ethical behaviour and through that, establishing and maintaining trust relationships with clients."

---

24   As of October 2015.

Creating shareholder value is essentially about building a sustainable competitive advantage – it's the reason clients consistently prefer to buy from one organisation rather than another. The way to do this is by playing open cards, and being transparent and ethical in everything you do.

A mission-driven, value-centred organisation is able to motivate employees to create innovative products and superior client service that is sustainable over a long period. This in turn leads to increased client satisfaction and a competitive advantage that drives high revenue growth, with high profit margins and high rates of growth in profitability. An organisation that proves to be profitable and sustainable will also prove to be commercially viable. Ultimately, this upward spiral of success attracting success, contributes to a positive impact on the organisation's overall reputation.

Transparency plays an important role in reputation management. Organisations face increasing pressure to report publicly, not just on financial performance but also on non-financial, social, environmental and ethical performance, and on remuneration policies. This reporting is becoming increasingly more specific and measurable and more subject to independent scrutiny and audit.

A reputation for high levels of transparency and frequency of information disclosure are therefore crucial to enable investors to make choices between various shares, bonds and other financial instruments. Without such transparency, investors are cautious because they are uncertain about what they are buying into.

Einwiller and Will[25] assert that although organisations have to be aware of the needs of all stakeholders, some stakeholders are more important than others. They view the financial community as the most important stakeholder group for the organisation and thus for corporate branding efforts. Gary and Smeltzer[26] and McNaughton[27] agree that the impact of an organisation's reputation on the financial community is dramatic. A favourable reputation is regarded as a prerequisite to succeed in the global financial marketplace. Shareholders can ultimately give or withhold their approval of management through their votes. In addition, their decisions on buying and selling influence share prices. This has a direct and measurable impact on an organisation's share price.

However, O'Connor[28], Berman and Woods[29] as well as Grupp and Gaines-Ross[30] concur that it is widely accepted that traditional accounting models provide an inadequate means of reflecting true share value. Historically, the value of intangible assets was considered relatively modest compared with tangible assets such as buildings, inventory and equipment. The differences between book value, net assets and share price can only be bridged by a more meaningful risk assessment of those factors that affect reputation. In today's fast-changing, knowledge-based economy, intangible assets

---

25 Einwiller and Will, *loc. cit.*

26 Gary, E.R. and Smeltzer, L.R. 1985. SMR Forum: Corporate Image – An Integral Part of Strategy. *Sloan Management Review*, 26(4):73-79.

27 McNaughton, *loc. cit.*

28 O'Connor, *loc. cit.*

29 Berman and Woods, *loc. cit.*

30 Grupp and Gaines-Ross, *loc. cit.*

such as brand strength, client relationships, intellectual property and human capital can make up a large portion of an organisation's value. It has been estimated that intangible assets can provide three times as much value as tangible assets.

Reducing stock market volatility by identifying and valuing unrecorded intangible assets could bolster organisational stability. A more inclusive reporting system would enhance operational capability and enable rationalisation of organistional strategy to occur, which is critical to managing reputation and share price. Accounting for broader social and ethical organisational practices could not only improve transparency and accountability with stakeholders; it could also limit scope for malpractice such as insider trading.

Share price can be directly related to shareholder value.

SHAREHOLDER VALUE

The shareholder value principle, according to Doyle[31] and Froud, Haslam, Johal and Williams in Morgan and Takahashi[32], holds that a business should be run to maximise the return on the shareholders' investment. The heart of shareholder value analysis is measuring whether the organisation has earned more than its weighted average

---

31   Doyle, *op. cit.*, p. 20.
32   Morgan, G. and Takahashi, Y. 2002. Shareholder Value in the Japanese Context. *Competition & Change*, 6(2):169-191.

cost of capital in any one year. From a shareholders' point of view, this is an indicator of whether they could earn more by putting capital into money accounts rather than taking a risk on shares.

Creating shareholder value is essentially about establishing a sustainable competitive advantage. External dialogue through marketing thus provides the tools for creating this competitive advantage. Mitchell[33] concurs and adds that the only way to maximise shareholder value is by delighting clients and motivating employees.

The discourse on shareholder value, according to Morgan and Takahashi[34], is crucially important to organisations and investors on a number of levels. It expresses the dominance of a particular set of shareholder interests in the process of managing the organisation. In theory, an organisation that does not deliver shareholder value[35] should see its share price fall as investors sell. However, where failure to achieve shareholder value is perceived to have occurred because of poor management, the organisation's share price will fall and this will lead to it becoming vulnerable to takeover.

This specific metric of shareholder value analysis provides investors with a way of deciding which organisations are providing them

---

33 Mitchell, A. 2002. Will the real shareholder value please stand out? *Marketing week*, 25(28):28-30.

34 Morgan and Takahashi, *loc. cit.*

35 Whatever metric is being used, this means that the organisation does not achieve higher returns than the average cost of capital.

with value, as the comparative yardstick is already built into the measure. It then becomes the basis for action in the capital markets. Metrics act as disciplinary devices on management through the mechanism of trading in the stock and bond markets. On the basis of these metrics, investors move funds around the marketplace, on the aggregate weakening some organisations and strengthening others. This occurs most clearly in relation to share price but also in terms of the interest rates and conditions on short-, medium- and long-term borrowing. The pressure for shareholder value is therefore translated into a measurable form, which acts as a disciplinary force on management and strategies of organisation growth and development.

Rajaji[36] comments that there is no single metric that can be used on an operational level to measure shareholder value. It is a high-level, multifaceted and long-term concept, and there is no single number one can use to guide decision-making. The best way to measure shareholder value is to break it down into a series of smaller-scale metrics that, put together in the right proportions, demonstrate shareholder value. Guidelines requiring executives to own a large number of shares in their organisations do not necessarily translate into better shareholder returns. The bottom line is therefore that shareholder value is a long-term notion that is very complex to compute. Short-term indicators such as revenue, share price and

---

36   Rajaji, R. 2002. Lessons in Shareholder Value; To deliver real value to the business, CIOs must make all investment decisions with the organisation's long-term goals in mind. *CIO Framingham*, 15(16):58-63.

growth do not necessarily say anything about shareholder value, especially when looked at in isolation.

Attractive shareholder value through the creation of competitive advantage will influence investors positively to invest in an organisation.

INVESTOR ATTRACTIVENESS

Haller and Boyd[37] comment that the primitive investor automatically assumes that an organisation with entries in many growth markets is a winner. The more pragmatic investor recognises growth markets as a double-edged sword – on one hand, it is important to be in them otherwise the business has no future; on the other hand, they usually produce negative cash flows. Hence, being in too many growth markets at the same time can spell disaster.

Antunovich, Laster and Mitnick[38] note that individuals and organisations investing in the stock market often prefer to buy shares of high-quality or blue-chip organisations. Some asset managers advocate a policy of investing exclusively in shares of leading organisations. Investors who favour the glamour shares of well-managed organisations argue that these organisations experience superior growth and profitability, which ultimately translate into

---

37   Haller and Boyd, *op. cit.*, p. 170.

38   Antunovich, P., Laster, D. & Mitnick, S. 2000. Are high-quality firms also high-quality investments? *Current Issues in Economics and Finance*, 6(1): 1-6.

superior share price performance. A high-quality organisation is indeed a high-quality investment.

Buying shares in organisations with fast sales growth and attractive prospects has proved especially popular with investors. Academic research, however, argues that glamour shares are unlikely to yield unusually high returns. Investors are willing to accept more modest returns from investing in high-quality organisations because these organisations pose a lower level of risk. Lakonishok, Shleifer and Vishny in Antunovich et al.[39] speculate that investors may accept a smaller return because they derive pleasure from owning shares of blue-chip organisations. Doyle[40] states that the value of an organisation measures the perceptions of professional investors on the ability of the organisation's leadership to master and manage this changing market environment. When investors perceive an organisation to be stuck in unattractive markets and lacking a competitive advantage, they naturally do not want to invest. The value of the organisation then declines, making it difficult for the organisation to attract resources and making it susceptible to being acquired.

The key to economic value creation is the organisation's ability to achieve or maintain competitive advantage in a changing market environment. To some extent, attracting investors to an organisation is driven by the organisation's profitability.

---

39   Antunovich *et al.*, *op. cit.*, p. 170.
40   Doyle, *op. cit.*, p. 15.

PROFITABILITY

When you are in business, you do so to make money and ultimately a profit.

According to Schwartz[41] and Kitson and Campbell in Fisher[42], a good organisation is profitable. If it is not profitable, it is not in business and it will not survive. La Berge and Svendsen in Testa[43] add that relationships lie at the heart of corporate profit making and sustainability in today's global economy.

George[44] states that a mission-driven, value-centred organisation is able to motivate employees to create innovative products and superior client service that is sustainable over a long period. This in turn leads to increased client satisfaction and a competitive advantage that drives high revenue growth, with high profit margins and high rates of growth in profitability.

In today's interlinked world, as described by Mastal[45], corporate reputation, which is the cumulative perceptions of an organisation by its key stakeholders, is increasingly recognised for its bottom-line impact. In fact, a large body of research shows that organisations with good reputations achieve higher-than-average profitability

41 Schwartz, P. 2000. When good companies do bad things. *Strategy and Leadership*, 28(3):4-11.
42 Fisher, *loc. cit.*
43 Testa, *loc. cit.*
44 George, *loc. cit.*
45 Mastal, *loc. cit.*

compared to their peers. Therefore, reputation ultimately has an influence on the organisation's sustainability.

ORGANISATIONAL SUSTAINABILITY

To be competitive, to survive and to grow in the market, according to Van der Walt et al.[46] the organisation must have competitive advantages. In all cases, the advantage must be sustainable over a certain period. A sustainable competitive advantage can be defined as the ability to deliver superior value to the market for a protracted period of time. Sustainable competitive advantages are necessary to out performthe competition.

Barney in Kowalczyk and Pawlish[47] adds that an organisation with a positive reputation can enjoy a significant competitive advantage, whereas an organisation with a negative reputation, or no reputation, may have to invest significant amounts over long periods to match the differentiated organisation.

An organisation that proves to be profitable and sustainable will also prove to be commercially viable.

---

46   Van der Walt *et al.*, *loc. cit.*
47   Kowalczyk and Pawlish, *loc. cit.*

COMMERCIAL VIABILITY

Grupp and Gaines-Ross[48] explain that calculating a return on investment (ROI) puts a financial value on achieving the organisational objective, which is usually revenue. Corporate reputation becomes increasingly dependent on an organisation's ability to execute an organisational model. Successful execution results in a good reputation, and correlates highly with strong financial performance and overall success. Therefore, a favourable organisation reputation delivers financial payoffs. Corporate reputation correlates with financial performance and return on investment.

TRANSPARENCY

Christensen[49] and Mayo[50] articulate that organisations face increasing pressure to report publicly, not just on financial performance, but also on non-financial, social, environmental and ethical performance, and on remuneration policies. In turn, reporting of non-financial performance is becoming increasingly more specific and measurable, and more subject to independent scrutiny and audit. While advertising standards and the law provide some regulation of the standards of reporting, the challenges remain to keep the focus on substance as well as form and to balance law and best practice.

---

48   Grupp and Gaines-Ross, *loc. cit.*
49   Christensen, L.T. 2002. Corporate communication: the challenge of transparency. Corporate communications: *An International Journal*, 7(3):162-168.
50   Mayo, *op. cit.*, p. 1.

There seems to be, according to Christensen[51], an implicit assumption in the literature that external stakeholders in general want or even demand organisational transparency. As Fombrun and Rindova in Christensen[52] point out, a primary mechanism for achieving transparency is expressive communication with stakeholders. This expressiveness is organised around the organisation's identity. If internal and external audiences agree on interpretations, in effect, there is transparency. Since this transparency is established through communication, external stakeholders demand more and more communication. Bickerton[53] postulates that communication benefits may result not only from the number and frequency of communications, but from the variety of issues about itself that an organisation reveals through its communications. Communication that creates transparency enables shareholders to appreciate the organisation's operations better, and so facilitate ascribing it a better reputation.

South Africans in particular are becoming fed up and are taking a stand against corruption and questionable business practices through campaigns such as Corruption Watch[54]. Sadly, bribery and corruption is still rife. Personally, I have found it surprising how questionable and quite blatant some business people are when it comes to conducting business.

---

51 Christensen, *loc. cit.*

52 *ibid.*

53 Bickerton, D. 2000. Corporate reputation versus corporate branding: the realist debate. *Corporate communications*, 5(1):42–48.

54 www.corruptionwatch.org.za

Interestingly, I was approached by someone to work on a tender with them; I have no problem in essence with tenders – let's face it, the government needs all the help they can get, they can't do everything alone. I also have no problem working in partnership or as a joint venture, especially when you can leverage off each other's strengths. However, my integrity radar started bleeping when I was presented with the tender documents before it went public. When I asked about this, I got "no comment" with a jovial laugh. As lovely as the project would have been, we gracefully bowed out to keep our integrity intact.

Pruzan[55] comments that perhaps the single major characteristic that accounting reports share is that almost all are either centre on the concept of stakeholder dialogue or profess that they will in the future. They are not just one-way communications prepared by experts – almost all the reports invite the stakeholders to participate in the development of the reports, the methodology employed and the development of new actions to improve corporate performance. In other words, rather than being solely based on management's perceptions of what is important to measure and on 'objective' measures of performance, the reports also focus on the values and aspirations of the various parties who affect and/or are affected by the organisation's decisions and actions.

Anon.[56] notes that organisations that release these financial results earlier than their industry peers achieve an average 15.5%

---

55   Pruzan, *loc. cit.*

56   Anon. 2003. *loc. cit.*

premium in their price-to-earnings ratio. De Chernatony[57] as well as Einwiller and Will[58], comment that the possibility for every stakeholder to access almost any information directed at other stakeholder groups, for example clients or activists accessing investor information, has led to much greater transparency than ever before. The consequences of these new possibilities are evident: any contradiction in what is being communicated to different stakeholder groups can be unveiled without much effort.

Apart from information conveyed by the organisation itself, Kartalia in Nakra[59] comments that the increased availability of corporate information via the Internet enhances the organisation's transparency. The plethora of Internet sources available includes independent sites for corporate information, client communities, anti-corporate sites and discussions in newsgroups, to mention only a few.

Morgan and Takahashi[60] postulate that, as critical accounting research has revealed, financial accounting is not simply a reflection of an underlying reality, it constitutes that reality by giving it a particular shape and form of visibility to both insiders and outsiders. In this sense, the claim of shareholder value discourse to create an objective measure of performance based on the transparency of organisation accounts is spurious because all accounting systems

---

57   De Chernatony, *op. cit.*, p. 106.

58   Einwiller and Will, *loc. cit.*

59   Nakra, *op. cit.*, p. 105.

60   Morgan and Takahashi, *loc. cit.*

are constructs with various forms of biases that can be exploited by corporate management. High levels of transparency and frequency of information disclosure are therefore crucial to enabling investors to make choices between various shares, bonds and other financial instruments. Without such transparency, investors are cautious because they are uncertain about what they are buying into.

The information released to outside investors drives the internal process of information collection and analysis. The shareholder value discourse is integrally related to the ability of managers to engage in rapid and major organisational restructuring in order to respond quickly to poor figures.

Anon.[61] notes that it is essential for organisations to make shareholder value a key management goal to improve competitiveness and to push for greater transparency and corporate governance. Investors appreciate the value of more comprehensive information from organisations as this helps them evaluate future financial performance. To attract capital, organisations need to understand the importance of good corporate governance and focus on areas that create shareholder value, which employs both financial and non-financial information.

---

61   Anon., *loc. cit.*, [5]

RELATIONSHIP WITH SHAREHOLDERS

Antunovich *et al.*[62] state that the relationship between corporate reputation and share returns suggests that reputation plays an important long-term role in shaping investment results.

Austin[63] notes that investors often ignore environmental issues at their own peril. An organisation's environmental performance is relevant not just for shareholders wishing to invest responsibly, but for any shareholder interested in return on investment. Environmental issues can have a significant influence on an organisation's bottom line and share price, and do impact on corporate reputation.

FINANCIAL MANAGEMENT'S INFLUENCE ON CORPORATE REPUTATION

Klein[64] asserts that the motivation to rush to reputation management and measurement is evidence that a good reputation can dramatically affect an organisation's results. Psychologically, an organisation with a solid reputation earns the benefit of the doubt in times of crisis. Good communication professionals know that a great deal is at stake in protecting and enhancing corporate

62   Antunovich *et al.*, *loc. cit.*

63   Austin, D. 2002. Environmental Risks Could Reduce Shareholder Value of Oil and Gas Companies. *Energy User News*, 27(9):42.

64   Klein, P. 1999. Measure what matters. *Communication World*, 16(i9):32.

reputation, especially in terms of building and maintaining relationships with stakeholders.

Financial management such as balance sheets and income statements are acknowledged to form a major portion of the aspects that influence investment decisions and corporate reputation. However, it is important to understand that these factors should not be viewed in isolation when a perception of an organisation is formed. Investor decisions are also driven strongly by corporate marketing and corporate communication.

SHAREHOLDER VALUE'S INFLUENCE ON CORPORATE REPUTATION

Corporate reputation is a very important asset for an organisation. According to Paster in Donlon[65], people sometimes confuse financial performance and reputation. Financial performance is very important, as are values and the manner in which stakeholders are dealt with and communicated to. Corporate image is particularly valuable in terms of an organisation's ability to raise debt and equity capital. In 2000, Cooper in Bennett and Kottasz[66] suggested that between 8% and 15% of an organisation's share price can be ascribed to corporate reputation. Antunovich et al.[67] concur that the relationship between corporate reputation and share

---

65 Donlon, op. cit., p. 50.
66 Bennett, R. and Kottasz, R. 2000. Practitioner perceptions of corporate reputation: an empirical investigation. Corporate communications, 5(4):224-234.
67 Antunovich et al., loc. cit.

returns suggests that reputation plays an important long-term role in shaping investment results.

In Deliotte's 2014 global survey on reputational risk[68], they indicate that according to a study by the World Economic Forum, on average more than 25% of a company's market value is directly attributable to its reputation.

Nakra[69] maintains that successful global leaders earn a reputation for credibility among investors by showing profitability to individual and institutional shareholders, maintaining a stable return on investment and nurturing financial growth prospects.

TRUSTWORTHINESS

Anderson in Bennett and Gabriel[70] as well as Raj[71] note that a trustworthy relationship is one in which a partner wishes to make a long-term commitment.

Trust is an important feature of any relationship. It creates the conditions under which commitment develops and organisations become willing to make relationship-specific investments capable

68   Deloitte. 2014. 2014 global survey on reputation risk: Reputation@Risk. www.deloitte.com/reputationrisksurvey. Viewed 29/10/2015

69   Nakra, *loc. cit.*

70   Bennett, R. and Gabriel, H. 2001. Reputation, trust and supplier commitment: The case of shipping organisation/seaport relations. *The Journal of Business & Industrial Marketing*, 16(6/7):424-438.

71   Raj, *loc. cit.*

of developing competitive advantage. Trust hinges on the belief that one partner will act in the best interests of the other. It is, however, important to note that trust in a partner is only likely to grow gradually, normally in small incremental stages. Metcalfe in Bennett and Gabriel[72] comment that the longer the period of exposure to a satisfactory partner, the higher the level of trust, with consequent willingness to undertake relationship-specific investments.

Richardson and Bolesh[73] state that reputable organisations protect their corporate reputations by maintaining high standards of practice no matter the circumstances. The most admired organisations use commitment to quality products and services to build and maintain their reputations.

ORGANISATIONAL SUSTAINABILITY'S INFLUENCE ON CORPORATE REPUTATION

Kowalczyk and Pawlish[74] mention that ultimately, reputations have economic value to organisations because they are difficult to imitate. Rivals simply cannot replicate the unique features and intricate processes that produced those reputations. Reputations are therefore a source of competitive advantage. Sustaining that relative

---

72   Gabriel, *op. cit.*, p. 424.
73   Richardson and Bolesh, *loc. cit.*
74   Kowalczyk and Pawlish, *loc. cit.*

advantage requires commitment to the ongoing management of an organisation's reputation.

Davies *et al.*[75] note that many existing approaches to the measurement of corporate reputation have been criticised as being overly focused on the financial performance of organisations and on the views of external stakeholders. Therefore, when corporate reputation is measured, the organisation's financial management must not be viewed in isolation. Other business processes, such as human resources, operations, information technology (IT) and corporate communication, also need to be taken into consideration. These processes are evaluated when using the Repudometer research tool.

》 **Things to consider when building your reputation through business results**

» Be transparent in all your dealings, especially financial ones.

» Ethical behaviour is non-negotiable on all levels of the business.

» Continuously build value for your shareholders.

» Shareholder value is maximised by delighting clients and motivating employees.

» Pricing is an important element to generating income.

---

75 Davies, G., Chun, R., da Silva, R.V. & Roper, S. 2001. The personification metaphor as a measurement approach for corporate reputation. *Corporate Reputation*, 4(2):113-127.

» Reputation management is not only dependent on financial results and profitability; there needs to balance in all business operations.

| CHAPTER 6 |

CORPORATE DIALOGUE

"When you know better you do better."

Maya Angelou

Van der Walt *et al.*[1] and Dowling in Christensen and Askegaard[2] explain external dialogue as an attempt by the organisation to project its 'ideal self-image' to both internal and external stake-holders, which will have an impact on corporate reputation.

The glue that binds all of these building blocks together and is the core of building the corporate reputation is *Corporate Dialogue*. This dimension is made up of *Internal Dialogue* in terms of change

---

1 Van der Walt *et al.*, *loc. cit.*

2 Christensen, L.T. and Askegaard, S. 2001. Corporate identity and corporate image revisited - A semiotic perspective. *European Journal of Marketing*, 35(3/4):292-31.

management and using the most appropriate channels of communication within the organisation to engage with the employees. Employee relations and team dynamics are measured to gauge what the employees' perceptions are of the organisation. As mentioned earlier in Chapter

5, employees play a critical role in the creation of an organisation's reputation. *External Dialogue* looks at engagement with stakeholders outside the organisation, be it through media liaison, marketing, public relations activities or social media engagement. Linked to external communication is stakeholder satisfaction and loyalty. Whatever is communicated both internally and externally, it is important that messages resonate with the overall strategic intent of the business.

Consistency is key in building a reputation. Davis and Dunn[3] say that organisations have to strive for competent, consistent and professional interaction with clients at all times, regardless of how and where the interaction is taking place.

---

3   Davis and Dunn, *loc. cit.*

DIALOGUE

Gotsi and Wilson[4] note that employees and their behaviour represent the reality of the organisation to the clients. If their behaviour does not live up to the expectations created through the organisation's external communication campaigns, the organisation's overall reputation will be damaged. Bernstel[5] comments that an organisation cannot deliver on its brand promise if the employees do not know or care about it. A successful organisation focuses on taking care of employees. Employee morale has an effect on everything, from frontline service to negative word-of-mouth. That is why aligning internal dialogue with strategic intent is so crucial.

Anon.[6], Harris and De Chernatony[7] and Davies and Chun[8] all agree that if employees express negative views about their organisation or, if what they say does not reflect the image the organisation is trying to project through its advertising, friends will believe the employees rather than the publicity. Organisations need to ensure that there is no gap between what the organisation is saying in the outside world and what people believe inside the business. Mastal[9] agrees that employees are 'brand ambassadors' and only if they 'live the brand' will reputation management efforts succeed.

---

4   Gotsi and Wilson, *loc. cit.*
5   Bernstel, J.B. 2003. Inner Branding. *Bank Marketing*, 35(3):14-19.
6   Anon. 2002. *loc. cit.*
7   Harris and De Chernatony, *loc. cit.*
8   Davies and Chun, *op. cit.*, p. 147.
9   Mastal, *loc. cit.*

Isn't it interesting that for the first time in the history of the business world, we have at least three generations that are all working together, the Baby Boomers, Generation X and Generation Y (also known as Millennials), all of whom require different modes of engagement. Navigating through the different characteristics, values, and attitudes toward work, based on the generation's life experiences can be like navigating a minefield. Getting it right and aligning your key messages internally are intrinsic to building a solid reputation. To successfully integrate these diverse generations into the workplace, companies need to embrace radical changes in recruitment, benefits, and creating a corporate culture that actively demonstrates respect and inclusion for its multigenerational work force.

All the departments need to work really closely with the internal Communication and human resources departments to maximise communication efforts and to make sure that messages are sent through the most appropriate channel of communication, interpreted correctly and that the required actions are taken. The way in which you communicate and get the most out of a Baby Boomer, is quite different with a Millennial. It is important to note that there is no right or wrong way of communicating, it's about being able to adapt to be most effective.

It is important to look at different communication strategies to successfully integrate the multigenerational work force. Why is this important for your reputation?

Employees play a vital role in the reputation of an organisation. Very often, this is where the reputation of an organisation starts, as their daily perceptions and interactions become the reality for external stakeholders. If the behaviour of employees does not live up to the expectations created through the organisation's external communication campaigns, the organisation's overall reputation will be damaged. What we have found is that if your employees' morale is low, then this generally has a negative impact on how the organisation is seen. Even if the external stakeholders do not regularly interact with the employees, they will pick up that there is something wrong.

I am stereo-typical and unashamedly Generation X; give me a laptop or Smartphone to hide behind, and I will conquer the world with e-mails and social networking. This, however, does not work when I need to engage with Baby Boomers – a quick face-to-face meeting or telephone call; in other words, verbal communication gets a lot of things ticked off the to-do list. Many of the Reputation Matters team are Millennials – a WhatsApp or text message generally sorts out a lot of things really quickly.

The key is to be flexible. You need to be able to effectively address and take advantage of the differences in values and expectations of each generation. That said, it is important not to follow blanket stereotypes. However, generalisations or broad overviews do help us be a little bit more understanding and tolerant of each other. Below is a guide to provide insight into each generation and how best to customise your communication.

Very broadly, this is how the different generations have been explained to me:

Baby Boomers (born 1943–1964) were the first generation to actively declare a higher priority for work over personal life. They generally distrust authority and large systems. This generation is the 'Me Generation', with its pursuit of personal gratification, which often shows up as a sense of entitlement in today's work force. Other characteristics include team involvement and personal growth. Traditionally, again generalising, the Baby Boomers in South Africa enjoy a good old 'bosberaad' or 'lekgotla' session – in other words, going away somewhere out of town for a day or two. The time is dedicated to the management team sitting around a table strategising the mission and vision, many notes are documented on flip charts, and generally this is all followed by some or other team building activity or two with a lot of socialising after a hard day of planning the future of the organisation. Then once everyone is back in the office, someone types up the notes, which get circulated to the rest of the organisation. So, pretty much a "This is what we decided, you need to implement it".

Even though Baby Boomers are becoming more technologically savvy, slowly but surely navigating their way around smartphones and realising that Facebook is not the scourge of the youth, they prefer face-to-face interaction and would much rather engage directly with someone. You will also find that this generation is a lot more likely to pick up the phone and make a call than depend on an e-mail. They're pretty competitive, open and direct. They want details. They don't want you to tell them what to do, they just want the information to make decisions.[10]

Tips for communicating to a Baby Boomer – direct interaction, be it in a meeting, strategy session or phone call.

Generation X (born 1965–1977) are more likely to be sceptical and independent-minded. Don't ask them to network – they are generally the first people to take out their laptops at a meeting, using it as a shield between them and other people. They grew up in an era when both parents were generally working. In other words, when they came home from school, they fended for themselves; they also became known as latch-key kids. They would then plonk themselves in front of the television, before, or while they did homework.

This generation naturally questions authority figures and are responsible for creating the work/life balance concept. Because Gen Xers place a lower priority on work, many company leaders from the Baby Boomer generation assume these workers are not as dedicated. However, Generation Xers are willing to develop their skill sets and take on challenges, and are perceived as very adaptive to job instability.

---

10   Nathan Solheim. 2012. *How to communicate with baby boomers.*
      http://www.benefitspro.com/2012/07/10/how-to-communicate-with-baby-boomers
      Viewed 29/10/2015

This is the first generation that had e-mail and other forms of electronic communications. They would much rather send an e-mail than have direct interaction such as a phone call.

Work/life balance is very important to this generation. Therefore, they prefer an e-mail so that they can tend to it when it suits their schedule.

Tips for communicating with a Generation Xer – send a text or e-mail so that they can respond when it fits into their timetable and speaks to their quest and need for work/life balance.

Generation Y (Millennials: born 1980–2000), are the technological whiz kids and are all about 'Why?' They are predicted to occupy almost half the working population by 2020. They are a lot more socially conscious and generally don't mind engaging and doing things as long as the 'Why' is explained to them. This group is the first global-centric generation, having come of age during the rapid growth of the Internet and an increase in global terrorism. They are among the most resilient in navigating change while deepening their appreciation for diversity and inclusion. They would far prefer to engage with people on social media than face to face. This generation is totally comfortable with digital technology and are excellent multi-taskers and the most team-centric generation.

At the same time, they are all about sharing and networking because most were raised in a time defined by boundary-less communication. For this reason, they naturally thrive in collaborative, open-space offices and e-mail threads with double digit

CC's. A flat organisational structure is preferred because everyone is equal.

They have grown up at a time when parents programmed much of their lives with sports, music, and recreational activities to keep them occupied[11], all the while sending text messages – they are impatient and require instant gratification as they have always had all the information they need at their fingertips via the Internet.

The typical Generation Yer is smart, creative, productive and achievement-oriented, and needs to work in a constantly stimulating environment with opportunities to develop their skills. They seek personal growth, meaningful careers, and mentors or supervisors to encourage and facilitate their professional development.

They have been constantly surrounded by choice, so don't tend to stay in one job for very long. If they don't get constant stimulation, they will walk out the door – in other words, they are not very loyal to companies if they feel that their needs are not being met. According to demographer Bernard Salt, the financial sector was seeing a 25% turnover of Gen Y staff each year. However, the global financial crisis has forced them to stay put in their jobs a little longer. Provided with rewards, access to training and inspiring leadership,

---

11   American Management Association. 2014. *Leading the Four Generations at Work.* http://www.amanet.org/training/articles/Leading-the-Four-Generations-at-Work. aspx. Viewed 29/10/2015

this generation will thrive and be the one to take business through to the future.[12]

You'll have your work cut out for you if you expect them to attend a 'bosberaad' without a compelling reason why it can't be done virtually. Also, don't just bring the notes back from a strategy session, and expect them to embrace the decisions made. Include them in the process; better yet, to get the most out of this group, host a webinar or a virtual meeting on one of the many platforms or apps available today.

With significant gains in technology and an increase in educational programming during the 1990s, the Millennials are also the most educated generation of workers today.

Texting or instant messaging became the preferred method of communications. Like Generation X their preferred communication is writing, however writing changed from e-mails to the short-hand writing of text messages,[13] the bane of many Baby Boomers and Generation Xers.

Open up the office. Millennials generally don't work well under rigid management structure. They prefer open collaborations that allow employees to share information and for everybody to contribute

---

12   CareerFAQs. 2014. *Workplace warfare: Baby Boomers, Gen X and Gen Y.*
     http://www.careerfaqs.com.au/news/news-and-views/workplace-warfare-baby-
     boomers-gen-x-and-gen-y. Viewed 29/10/2015

13   Mark Miller. 2013. *Generational Communication Style.*
     https://careerpivot.com/2013/communication-style-generational-workplace.
     Viewed 29/10/2015

to decision-making. Assign work to teams of employees and have them present the finished product to the entire department. The idea is to take advantage of the Millennials' preference for teamwork and to encourage more solidarity throughout the workplace.

Tips for communicating to Generation Y: Remember, this is the 'Why?' generation, so make sure that you are armed with sufficient reasons when decisions are made. Work together as a group to come up with solutions. They prefer to communicate through platforms such as e-mail, Instant Messaging (IM), blogs and text messages, rather than on the phone or face to face. Gen Y also prefers cyber-training, web-based delivery systems and telecommuting rather than traditional lectures or training.

What about **Generation Z**? Set to occupy roughly 10% of the workforce by 2020, experts predict that with this generation there will be a return to values such as respect, responsibility and restraint. However, with the way technology is heading, most of the jobs that Gen Z will be filling have not even been created yet![14]

---

14   CareerFAQs, *loc. cit.*

CHANGE MANAGEMENT

> *"Motivation is the art of getting people to do what*
> *you want them to do because they want to do it."*
>
> DWIGHT D. EISENHOWER

Change management can be defined as "the coordination of a structured period of transition from situation A to situation B in order to achieve lasting change within an organisation":[15] It is about minimising resistance to organisational change through the involvement of key stakeholders[16]. Internal dialogue is an important driver of successful change within an organisation.

During times of change, stakeholders, especially employees, become incredibly stressed. Their core need is to know whether their jobs are secure. It is therefore very important that change management initiatives happen very early on in any changing scenario within an organisation. Sadly, communication and change management initiatives are introduced much too late in most change processes. By that time, doubt, rumours and a lack of trust in the system and management are rife.

I have been involved in many change management initiatives over the years, and more often than not, I have heard, "Oh dear, we

---

15   Mark Connelly. 2015. *Change Management Coach: What is Change Management?*
     http://www.change-management-coach.com/what-is-change-management.html
     Viewed 29/10/2015

16   Business Dictionary. 2015. *Change management.*
     http://www.businessdictionary.com/definition/change-management.
     html#ixzz3lmXMhGYh. Viewed 29/10/2015

should have started our communication months ago … now it is too late, and we need crisis management." It is understandable that you don't want to over-communicate about something that is as yet uncertain, to avoid unnecessary stress. However, if there is any possible change in the air, it will be sniffed out. If rumours are not nipped in the bud, you could have anarchy on your hands. Even if change is not imminent, it is still important to communicate it. Either way, keep your stakeholders informed about what is going on.

It is important to get the communication right. Very often, impending changes within an organisation will have a huge impact on the stakeholders and require them to do things in a different way. Ultimately, they will likely be required to change a behaviour and adopt a new way of doing things. It is important that the benefits of the change be communicated right from the start to obtain buy-in. A lot of time and resources will be wasted if there isn't buy-in into the new way of doing things, and people revert to their old ways of doing things.

An interesting project that I worked on many moons ago, was implementing an information-sharing repository for a large organisation. Mind sets had to be changed from printing out e-mails and documents and physically filing them away to saving the electronic documents in a central repository where the information could be shared and accessed by various departments.

You can just imagine the stress that this new system caused. Here you had someone who had quite diligently been printing and filing the documents away and in typical 'baby boomer' fashion been available to provide face-to-face feedback, training and mentorship in their specialist areas. Now the person was required to use technology to share information they had built up over a life time with all and sundry via a shared repository. The stress was palpable. They wondered whether their work was now going to be scrutinised by everyone. "If my information is shared with everyone, is there still going to be a need for my services if everyone has easy access to it?" "How safe is my position?" "How secure is the system?" "What happens if there is a breakdown in technology and all the work gets lost?" "I hate technology and don't trust computers – no thank you, I would rather continue to print it all out and have a backup system in place."

In change management, it is important to recognise where we are, in other words, the current situation (e.g. manually printing and filing documents) and to determine where we want to be, the desired destination (sharing all documents in a central repository). Once this is done, we need to identify the course of action to get from the current situation to the desired situation that will maximise buy-in and support for the end result. It is all about communicating the most appropriate message to the right audience through the most appropriate channels of communication. Communicating the rationale for the change and the impending implications is important. In addition, very importantly, the benefits of the end result and what new activities and roles will be expected from the stakeholders are key to the change management process. As an extreme and basic example, it would not have helped anyone had we let the employees know on the Friday that as of Monday they would have to start using the central repository.

Change management is a process, and people need to be transitioned from one reality to the next through communication and thorough planning. In other words, we had to let the employees know exactly what, where, when, how and what ongoing support they would be given to reach the desired destination, as well as the benefits of everyone reaching the change vision.

When it comes to change management initiatives, we need to use the most appropriate channels of communication, taking the three generations into consideration. In the area of information overload and 'death-by-e-mail' we need to look at ways of communicating through the clutter. Most large organisations have a plethora of channels they use to communicate with their employees – e-mails, an intranet, notice boards, newsletters, meetings, internal publications and road shows are just a few examples. During a change exercise, it is about using and maximising the communication channels available and not reinventing the wheel. That said, it is highly recommended to also look for alternative ways to get the message across – something that will cut through the noise and be noticed. Having a specific change management strategy and plan, and running it as a change campaign, will help to identify ways to pique interest and get creative about getting the message(s) across. Involving everyone throughout the process is very important – you are much more likely to get buy-in when you do engage in dialogue.

Something we have seen in our projects is the importance of giving employees a platform for feedback and dialogue during transitions – i.e. giving them a voice. Very often, larger organisations have so many policies and procedures in place to be a well-oiled machine that the human element has been forgotten. Because the employees are at the coal-face, they more often than not have incredibly good suggestions on what would or would not work, as they are integrally involved in a specific part of the business on a daily basis. Allowing employees to be intrepreneurial encourages the team to look for solutions to build the business. This then boosts employee morale and productivity, and builds the organisation. However, it is all good and well to give employees a voice, 'hearing' and acting on the voice of the employees are just as important.

CRITICAL SUCCESS FACTORS

» One of the very first lessons I learnt on my first change management project from my mentor at the time, was to determine the change vision, i.e. what is it that we want to achieve through the change. Using my previous example, the ultimate vision/ end result was to get everyone using and sharing information in a central repository. It is imperative that the change vision be aligned with the overall project, and ultimately business vision and objectives (strategic intent). Once the vision has been established, it needs to be incorporated into every piece of communication. This golden thread running throughout ensures that a consistent message is sent out. It is important that everyone understand where we are going and to obtain buy-in as early in the process as possible. However, as a change manager, brace yourself – it is not always a smooth journey.

» The next step is to identify the stakeholders you need to engage with. It is important to identify the internal stakeholders, top management, divisional managers, operators and so on. Determine how each group will be impacted by the change and decide how best to communicate the change to maximise their buy-in.

Buy-in from the leadership of the organisation is key. All the change initiatives should be agreed to and visibility supported by the executive of the organisation. Ultimately, they need to be seen implementing the change themselves. A comprehensive, proactive management plan needs to be in place. Referring to our example, if the executive of the organisation had not been seen to support the project and using the central repository there would be no reason for the rest of the team to follow-suit. If the boss could not be bothered to do it, why should I? Top-level buy-in as soon as possible is therefore really important in the change process.

Remember to also consider external stakeholders – would suppliers, partners, sponsors or even the media need to know about the change? If so, they need to be included in the change strategy and plan, and key messages developed for each group.

» **Readiness assessment** – once we know who we need to communicate to, we need to assess how ready they would be to embrace the change. This will impact the communication activities needed. In other words, someone who is very reluctant and not ready to change at all, will require very different communication in terms of messaging, channel and frequency of communication.

» **Trained change agents** should be included in the process. Change management is not rocket science, however, it is important that you have the right team in place to drive the process from start to finish. There needs to be an internal change management team as well as an independent, external team to keep things objective and to give a different perspective.

» **Identify Change Champions** – these are peers who buy into the process and then help to explain it to others and lead the way. Identify someone whose opinion is valued and get their buy-in.They will then help you to get your change message across. Interestingly, what worked really successfully in the project we've been discussing, was identifying a person who was actually quite negative and verbal about the project. He had been in the company for quite some time and his team had a high regard for him and respected his opinions. He made no secret about his disdain for the banality of the whole project. We then engaged with him in a one-on-one session to hear about his frustrations and used the opportunity to address the 'pain points'. We linked those to the end vision and resultant benefits the change would have, not only to the individual team members, but also the rest of the organisation. He was a hard nut to crack; however once he understood that no jobs were at stake, that sharing information would open other opportunities and ultimately save time, we could see the 'aha-moment' and had a change agent on our hands. He helped us to get his team and other divisions enthusiastic about the project, and actually wanting the process to move along more quickly.

» **Keep the momentum going** – it's all good and well to identify and get change agents on your side, however it is important to keep things moving. It would be quite counterproductive to get buy-in and excitement going … and then nothing happens. Not only will it negatively impact the support for the project but also all future change management programs. If people don't see things happening and changing then the chances of them believing you and buying into the next change will be much less likely.

» **Celebrate quick-wins** is another way to keep the momentum going – achievements within the project must be celebrated. What we did was identify small 'wins' throughout as well as bigger wins, such as reaching specific targets of people using the central repository.

» **Communication is key** and change initiatives must be focused and make an impact. Even if there is a lull in the project for whatever reason, keep stakeholders informed. Even if there is no movement, communicate any possible reason so that employees are kept in the loop. However, it is important not to communicate purely for the sake of communicating – all communication initiatives need to link back to achieving the end result. It is also important to communicate what will be done to empower individuals or teams to embrace the change, such as training and support. In our example, providing training on how the system works was really important. Post-training support was also important. People wanted to know that if they had a query they could pick up the phone and get the technical support they needed. We also had to communicate what backup systems were in place, how often documents would be backed up and what would happen to documents during a power outage so that employees had peace of mind when sharing their information. The benefit of sharing information is that the more you share, the more you get.

The ADKAR® Change Management Model[17] can be used quite effectively as a guide on what to include in the communication:

> **Awareness** – creating an awareness that change needs to take place. In other words, focus on the discomfort of the current situation and that change is imminent.

> **Desire** – creating a desire for the change to happen and calling on employees to participate in the process.

> **Knowledge** – providing information about the impact of the change. In other words, what does the changed situation look like?

> **Ability** – implementing the change on a day-to-day basis. In other words, focus on the training and support to be provided to employees to enable them to accept and implement the change.

---

17   Prosci Change Management Learning Center. 2007. *ADKAR: Change Management Model*. http://www.change-management.com/tutorial-adkar-overview.htm. Viewed 29/10/2015.

> › **Reinforcement** – keeping the change in place, reinforced with positive messages highlighting wins and profiling successes throughout the project.

» The change needs to be sustainable – it does not help if once the project has been rolled out people revert to their old ways of doing things. We want them to think, "How did we ever manage without this?" Change then becomes part of their normal daily activities.

Something to keep in mind throughout the change process is that we are all human beings, each with our own unique personality and emotional responses to situations. The five stages of normal grief as outlined by Elisabeth Kübler-Ross[18] in her 1969 book *On Death and Dying* should be considered when working on change management projects. This may seem incredibly drastic and morbid, however we need to keep in mind that when changes happen, people react to it differently. Very often, it is about letting go of the 'normal' way of doing things around here and accepting that things won't be the same.

Very briefly, these stages are:

» **Denial** – denying the reality of the situation. In other words, denying that the change will be taking place and carrying on with daily life as it is. Not believing that the change is imminent

---

18   Elisabeth Kübler-Ross. 1969. *On Death and Dying.* New York: The Macmillan Company.

and will happen. Denying that the new computer system/ central repository will be implemented.

» **Anger** – as the denial wears off and it becomes clear that the change is going to happen, reality sets in. People may become very angry about the situation and express frustration and resentment.

» **Bargaining** – looking for any possible way to make the situation work through negotiating or making threats. "I will do this IF..." scenarios come to the fore.

» **Depression** – can surface in many different forms.

» **Testing** – in change management, the step before Acceptance entails experimenting with the new system and seeing that it isn't as bad as you may have thought.

» **Acceptance** – accepting the change and making peace with having to do things differently.

It is important to note that everyone deals with change differently. This is not a set sequence; some people may jump from denial directly to depression, or go from anger to testing to bargaining before they accept the change.

⟩⟩ Things to consider when it comes to internal dialogue

» Employees like to have a voice and to be heard. Facilitate feedback opportunities through different forums.

» Be careful not to follow blanket stereotypes when communicating to different generations[19]. However, take into account that different generations have preferred working and learning requirements. This includes meetings and recognition programmes.

» Expand your communication strategies. Most companies rely too heavily on one strategy for corporate communication. By making the same message available in multiple formats, you'll ensure that you reach all employees.

» Make mentoring a constant. As your more established and experienced employees head toward retirement, develop strategies to ensure knowledge transfer and capture of organisational memory.

» Leaders must remain open to new ideas and provide constant feedback, working with managers and staff to shape the company's strategic vision. They must avoid projecting their own expectations about work and remain open to different perspectives based on generational attitudes.[20]

---

19   The Wall Street Journal How-To Guides: Managing your People. 2015. *How to Manage Different Generations*. http://guides.wsj.com/management/managing-your-people/how-to-manage-different-generations. Viewed 29/10/2015

20   American Management Association, *loc. cit.*

» When it comes to change management remember to:

> › Have a change vision.

> › Identify all the stakeholders that you need to communicate the change to.

> › Have top level buy-in and visibly seen embracing the change.

> › Identify change agents.

> › Have a comprehensive communication strategy and plan to support the change. Highlight how people will be impacted, what is required from them, and what training and support to provide.

> › Keep in mind that you are dealing with people who are emotional beings and take their state of mind into consideration.

EXTERNAL DIALOGUE

"If I was down to my last dollar, I'd spend it on Public Relations."

BILL GATES

Once your house is in order, you can start communicating to the outside world. It is highly recommended that you have the basic building blocks in place before you consider any external communication campaigns. It does not help to create greater awareness and get more sales queries, but your employees are not trained or

ready for the increase in production, or your processes aren't in place to ensure consistent delivery of products and services to cope with the increased demand. You will do a lot more damage to your reputation, and ultimately your back pocket, if you prematurely engage in promotions (external dialogue) such as advertising and media liaison (public relations) without having a solid foundation in place.

This is where research also plays a very important role. It is very important to understand which area of the business is of particular interest to which stakeholder group. In this way, you will be able to refine your communication strategy and plan accordingly, making sure that you communicate the most appropriate message(s) to the right audience using the most effective channels of communication for that group. Through your research, you may even identify areas that you assumed stakeholders knew about and now realise that there is a gap in communication. This gap may be negatively impacting your organisation's reputation, but constitutes an opportunity to communicate about new exciting developments that may be of interest to your stakeholders.

Zyglidopoulos and Phillips in Goldberg, Cohen and Fiegenbaum[21] comment that an organisation must be aware of the different concerns of various stakeholders when choosing a reputation-building strategy. Klein[22], Harris and De Chernatony[23] and Einwiller and Will[24] all agree that a good gauge of an organisation's reputation considers the views of all its different stakeholders. A good measurement of corporate reputation includes more than investors' views. De Seguna in Hanson and Stuart[25] as well as Einwiller and Will[26] state that in order to implement a system of reputation management, it is necessary to ensure that all stakeholders have a realistic image of what they can and cannot expect from an organisation. Creating a coherent perception of an organisation in the minds of its various stakeholders is a major challenge faced by many organisations. Incoherence in messages and difficulties in co-ordination are often fostered by communication representatives' narrow focus on their particular stakeholder groups. It is necessary to ensure that the organisation delivers what it promises and only promises to deliver what it can realistically undertake.

Nakra[27] notes that corporate reputation emanates from all the business activities and communications it undertakes intentionally

---

21 Goldberg *et al., loc. cit.*

22 Klein, *loc. cit.*

23 Harris and De Chernatony, *loc. cit.*

24 Einwiller and Will, *loc. cit.*

25 Hanson, D. and Stuart, H. 2001. Failing the reputation management test: The case of BHP. *The Big Australian Corporate Reputation Review*, 4(2):128-143.

26 *ibid.*

27 Nakra, *loc. cit.*

and unintentionally in the marketplace, such as advertising, promotion, direct marketing, personal selling, trade relations, public relations and community relations. Different stakeholders view a corporation differently because they regard particular areas of the organisation as being important. Saxton in Nakra[28] comments that all stakeholders, however, are affected by the brand image, and the corporate reputation created through advertising and other marketing communications activities.

So your building blocks are in place, and you are ready to make a noise about it – where to start?

1. **Stakeholders** – identifying who you want to communicate to and what you want them to do, i.e. buy your product or service, or gain more knowledge from your experience.

2. **Messages** – once you know who you want to speak to and what you want them to do, you can refine your messages accordingly. It is important to keep your strategic intent in mind when developing these messages. Also try to incorporate some type of call to action in the communication that you disseminate. For example, encourage people to invest in your products or services through an advert, or encourage people to visit your website for more information. Either way, have some metric in place to measure whether the message has been received, interpreted correctly and is being acted on – more sales, more visits to the website, more enquiries, and so on.

---

28   Nakra, *loc. cit.*

3. The **channel of communication** needs to be considered next. So once you know who you want to speak to and what you want to say to them, determine how best to engage with them. Factor in the generation preferences mentioned earlier. Remember that there is a lot of noise with all the information and brands competing for attention – consider what will make your brand stand out from the rest.

4. Have **feedback** mechanisms in place so that you do actually encourage dialogue with your stakeholders, otherwise the communication becomes very one-sided. This will help you discover what is working, what is not working and what is impacting your reputation. It will also confirm whether the messages and channels of communication themselves are working.

5. **Integrated communication** – the days of only advertising or only relying on a PR campaign are over. Integrating your message through all channels of communication, be it above the line (advertising), below the line (traditional PR), through social networking or your website, all need to be maximised and used in synergy for maximum effect.

INTEGRATED MARKETING COMMUNICATIONS

For years advertising has been seen as the be-all and end-all when communicating to external stakeholders. It still irks me when marketers think that reputation and communication management fall under the marketing umbrella. The long and the short of it is that advertising and marketing form a component in the external dialogue building block within the reputation management space. It is important to note that advertising and marketing can't be done in isolation – there needs to be a balance among the various communication options. With the economic crunch at the moment, companies are steering away from traditional advertising campaigns and are opting for more affordable communication options to engage with stakeholders, with social media platforms becoming the flavour of the day.

This is all good and well, and the more creative the better; however it is important to keep the basics of message, channel, audience and feedback in mind.

Miller in Donlon[29] suggests that one way to help reputation is to deal effectively with the media. The organisation needs to respond while the news is breaking, and not after there has been time to decide what is to be said. Mastal[30] notes that an organisation's message strategy should reflect its corporate position as well as the position it is taking on the issues. Organisations that have strong reputations generally have three or four key messages they recite over and over in all media and to all key stakeholders. That said, something to keep in mind, which was discussed at the recent International Public Relations Association (IPRA) Congress in Johannesburg (2015), is that spokespeople need to steer away from mechanically relaying a message. Storytelling is incredibly powerful and will

---

29 Donlon, *op. cit.*, p. 50.

30 Mastal, *loc. cit.*

resonate a lot more with your audience than stark, unemotional facts. Using a story to find a connection with your stakeholders will be a lot more powerful and encourage greater engagement than an impersonal relaying of a message.

The media, both traditional media (print, online, radio and television) and social media (LinkedIn, Facebook, Twitter, Instagram and blogs, to name a few of the thousands that exist) plays an important role in building or breaking down an organisation's reputation. It is important for organisations to understand how the media works and to build and foster this relationship.

When it comes to social media, it is important to identify which platforms are most appropriate for the organisation, and then determine a strategy and plan around it. Too often companies think that they need a Facebook and Twitter page without much thought or strategy around it. The pages are initially updated with great gusto only to lose momentum as other focus areas of the business become more important. Then, before they know it, it's been eight months since the last update. Then they decide that it is something for the younger generation to manage, so engage an intern to manage the social media posts. Social media needs to be strategic, aligned to your strategic intent and, ultimately, make sense to your target audience.

Taking a look at traditional media: Unless you are paying for advertising space, the media are not there to promote your brand. They are there to inform the public of news, industry developments, trends, opinions, and let's face it – scandal and disasters. It's third-party reporting because you are not paying for it, so editorial space and radio interviews are regarded considerably more credible than an advert. With an advert, you have total control over size, colour, wording and, if you are lucky, positioning. With editorial or an interview, you rely on the journalist to report accurately. It is therefore up to you to provide the journalist, producer or editor with the most appropriate (non-promotional) information, which is something they would want to share with their audience. It is also up to you to know how to get the best out of a print, radio or television journalist interview scenario.

With advertising, there is so much clutter to cut through, you need to advertise at minimum four times in the same channel to be seen. Just think about it – how often do you zone out or change the channel when there is a radio or television advert on? Or skim over a magazine ad? Wouldn't you agree that you are more likely to read an article or listen to an interview? Incidentally, marketers have cottoned on to this and are embracing content marketing, or paid-for editorial, which basically all boils down to advertorials. It looks like an 'independent' editorial piece but has actually been paid for. Personally I don't have much regard for advertorials as they are not credible at all. Rather invest in an integrated communication plan to reach out and engage with your stakeholders.

Getting back to traditional means of unpaid-for media coverage, media training should be non-negotiable for all executives and their teams. A media policy should also be in place and easily understandable and accessible to everyone. I mention teams because even though the majority of employees may never come close to being interviewed, it is really important that they understand how the media works. The last thing you want is for an over-eager receptionist to tell her version of a corporate rumour to a willing-to-listen journalist. Incidentally Donlon[31] warns that CEOs should take nothing for granted, particularly concerning their employees, as it is suggested that this is where the news media look first for ammunition when attacking an organisation or its products.

There are three key messages I always convey during our media training sessions. Firstly, there is no such thing as 'no comment' – that in itself is a comment. In fact everyone who hears that phrase jumps very quickly to their own conclusion and fills the gap with their own imagination.

Secondly, 'off the record' does not exist. Journalists get bombarded with so many media releases and information every day that a week from now they won't remember whether it was said on or off the record. Rule of thumb: If you don't want it to be known to the public, keep quiet. Warren Buffet has a wonderful quote: *"We must continue to measure every act against not only what is legal but also what we would be happy to have written about on the front page of a national newspaper in an article written by an unfriendly but intelligent reporter."*

Finally, incorporate your company name or contact details in the interview as far as possible. People may have missed the introduction and not heard where you are from, so use the opportunity to (subtly)

---

31   Donlon, *op. cit.*, p. 50.

bring in where you are from. It's quite frustrating when you are listening to a very interesting interview and you don't know where the person is from or where to start looking for more information.

Remember throughout to build a rapport with your audience. As mentioned earlier, it's about telling a story and not just regurgitating key messages.

I can't emphasise this enough – editorial or a radio interview (PR) is not going to get you more sales immediately. In other words, your phone is not going to start ringing off the hook once you've had a radio interview. Similarly, placing one advert in the local paper has the same lack of effect. You need to have an integrated communication strategy and plan in place. You need to keep the momentum going by working on different campaigns to raise awareness using different channels of communication and looking for different interesting angles to feed through to the media.

Media liaison (PR), is there to build credibility for your organisation. It is there to create public awareness of what you do, positioning you as an expert in your field (of course, you need to be!) and what it is that sets you apart. Then they will start seeking out your advice and ultimately your products and services. You first need to build a reserve of credibility before people will invest in you and your organisation. A reputation takes time to build.

"Many a small thing has been made large
by the right kind of advertising."
Mark Twain

VISUAL PRESENTATION OF THE ORGANISATION INFLUENCING CORPORATE IDENTITY

As mentioned throughout, there needs to be balance among all the dimensions of an organisation's reputation. As much as editorial and (positive) media exposure are important for any business, so too is the visual aspect of what the organisation portrays – in other words, its corporate identity. Again, it is important that the visual aspects of the business – the location of corporate head office and the logo/branding – are aligned to the overall business strategic intent and form an image stakeholders can resonate with. It also needs to be used consistently on all marketing collateral. Investing in a 'brand bible' of how to use the logo, including the dimensions, colours and placement is a really worthwhile investment if your brand is important to you. This will ensure that your brand looks the same from the letterhead right through to your website, and that it is used correctly on all communication disseminated by the organisation.

Van Heerden and Puth[32], Bennett and Kottasz[33] and Christensen and Askegaard[34] agree that corporate identity relates to the self-presentation of an organisation, and thus consists of the cues that it offers via its symbols, communications and other signals.

32 Van Heerden, C.H. and Puth, G. 1995. Factors that determine the corporate image of South African banking institutions an exploratory investigation. *International Journal of Bank Marketing*, 13(3):12-17.

33 Bennett and Kottasz, *loc. cit.*

34 Christensen and Askegaard, *loc. cit.*

ORGANISATION LOGO

Gary and Smeltzer[35] comment that some organisations are addressing the concept of identity by changing their logos. Such has been the influence of graphic design that it has almost become self-evident that any change of corporate identity will have an attendant change of visual identity. That said, it does not help going through a re-branding exercise if the other building blocks within your organisation are not addressed. Re-branding alone is not going to fix your business.

A visual audit may reveal symptoms of inherent corporate malaise. Many organisations fall into the trap of resorting to the initiation of a new visual identity as a means of correcting what may be profound organisational difficulties. This suggests a degree of naivety on the part of senior managers and consultancies in failing to differentiate between the causes and the symptoms of poor corporate identity. Balmer[36] comments on the importance accorded to graphic design in the corporate identity literature. Some writers with backgrounds in marketing and communication have accorded symbolism the same importance as other corporate identity elements such as behaviour.

The emphasis given to graphic design incorporate identity studies has been perpetuated by many so-called corporate identity con-

35   Gary and Smeltzer, *loc. cit.*
36   Balmer, J.M.T. 2001. Corporate identity, corporate branding and corporate marketing – Seeing through the fog. *European Journal of Marketing*, 35(3/4): 248-291.

sultancies, which are, to all intents and purposes, graphic design consultancies. This has had the unfortunate effect of stifling a broader, more sophisticated and scholarly appreciation of corporate identity. I don't refute that visual identification does, unquestionably, have power. Gary and Smeltzer[37] and Bromley[38] note that an organisation's visual identity is assumed to be a very important aspect of corporate communications. Logos may express an organisation's internal identity in terms of how its leaders conceptualise it, rather than its external image, which is how the organisation is perceived by others outside the organisation. Included in the contextualisation of a logo are the tangible and intangible elements that make any organisation distinct.

THE IMAGE OF AN ORGANISATION

Easton[39], Gary and Smeltzer[40], Bickerton[41] as well as Christensen and Askegaard[42] summarise that the corporate image is based on the collective impressions of all the stakeholders of the organisation. These impressions are derived from an organisation in its surroundings, such as a personal contact with the organisation, hearsay, mass media, communication media and psychological

---

37 Gary and Smeltzer, *loc. cit.*

38 Bromley, *op. cit.*, p. 73.

39 Easton, A. 1966. Corporate Style versus Corporate Image. *Journal of Marketing Research*, 3(2):168-175.

40 *ibid.*

41 Bickerton, *op. cit.*, p. 73.

42 Christensen and Askegaard, *loc. cit.*

predispositions not controlled by the organisation. All this relates to corporate management, specifically the corporate governance[43] element of having processes and policies in place, and the importance of consistency. This totality relates to how the organisation is perceived by all its stakeholders.

According to Davies *et al.*[44], image is taken to mean the view of the organisation held by external stakeholders. Ettorre[45] and O'Connor[46] acknowledge that there are many factors to consider when examining a corporate image, as it is very complex. The cross-functionality needed to sustain the good reputation of a corporate identity is central to management. Simply put, a client may be delighted with a product but may find the marketing material, the sales technique, the billing mechanism or the after sales care substandard.

In other words, corporate reputation needs to be managed and looked after by all the managers within the organisation, from human resources departments to IT and the finance offices. Everyone and every function within the organisation play a key role in how the organisation is perceived, and its resultant reputation.

---

43 See Chapter 2.
44 Davies *et al.*, *loc. cit.*
45 Ettorre, *loc. cit.*
46 O'Connor, *loc. cit.*

CORPORATE BRANDING

Bennett and Gabriel[47] and De Chernatony[48] note that reputation is an overall cognitive impression of an organisation based on its corporate branding and various marketing communication tools. A favourable reputation creates expectations of the organisation in terms of promises that are made to stakeholders and confers a competitive advantage in that it can help the organisation to survive occasional adverse publicity.

It is about building up a reputational credit bank to tap into, especially during a crisis. People tend to be more lenient towards organisations that have built up their reputational reserve over the years through their business practices and engagement with stakeholders than they are towards companies that people have hardly heard of or who have made no attempt to foster a relationship with them.

RELATIONSHIPS WITH STAKEHOLDERS

Davis and Dunn[49] say that it is important to remember that clients are complex and respond to situations, interaction and relationships on many different levels – emotional, intellectual, rational, intuitive and social. Richardson and Bolesh[50] add that clients respect

---

47   Bennett and Gabriel, *loc. cit.*

48   De Chernatony, *loc. cit.*

49   Davis and Dunn, *loc. cit.*

50   Richardson and Bolesh, *loc. cit.*

organisations they trust and two-way communication builds client confidence. To encourage interaction, organisations may develop listening posts through service centres, sales efforts and web-based programmes. Feedback forums and platforms are very important and have been made a lot easier by social media where customers are very vocal.

Actively listening to clients enhances an organisation's reputation for accessibility and accountability. Employees at all levels are attuned to feedback and use the information to address problems and secure happy clients. Active listening does not stop with acknowledgement of client comments, however. Reputable organisations use incoming data to shape strategy and identify improvement opportunities. Comments and criticism from real clients drives decisions on strategy, processes and product design.

Hall[51] notes that clients are the source of value and most organisations do not have a set of metrics that accurately reflects where value is being created and where it is being destroyed. If clients are the source of revenue, cash flow, profits and ultimately, equity, then it is crucial that all parties to the relationship, including shareholders, management, employees and clients, know where value is currently being created and destroyed, what is planned for in the future and how well it is working out. The value of research is therefore invaluable.

---

51   Hall, R. 2002. Linking customer and shareholder value. *Bank Marketing*, 34(6):9-10.

⟩⟩ Things to consider when it comes to external dialogue

» Invest in research and understand what is important to your stakeholders and how you measure up. This will provide you with valuable insights and help you to align your communication initiatives accordingly.

» The whole internal organisation impacts how it is seen externally.

» Know who your stakeholders are, refine your message(s) for each group and use the most appropriate channels of communication.

» Remember that it is about storytelling and not just about regurgitating the key messages.

» Have feedback mechanisms in place.

» Invest in media training for the whole team.

» There is no such thing as 'no comment' or 'off the record'; Remember to give your company's contact details during an interview, when possible, and remember to include a human element, i.e. a story.

» Have an integrated communication strategy in place, i.e. use a mixture of traditional media (editorials), advertising and social media.

» Align your corporate image to your strategic intent. Test and measure it to see if your stakeholders resonate with it.

» Align all your marketing collateral to have the same look and feel, invest in a 'brand Bible' to align your marketing collateral.

» Don't have a social media page just for the sake of it – if you do, steer away from the temptation of getting a newly appointed intern to manage it.

| CHAPTER 7 |

BUILDING A SOLID FOUNDATION

Bringing it all together: All the areas within the business that need to be taken into consideration when building your desired reputation are outlined in this chapter. These are not hard-and-fast rules; rather they form a guide of things to remember that may impact your organisation's reputation.

As mentioned throughout the book, all the dimensions of the reputation management foundation need to be in balance. If any of the areas within the business is out of kilter, it will negatively impact how the organisation is seen and the stability of your organisation's reputation. It is also important to remember that all of these dimensions are interlinked and not mutually exclusive. All areas of your business impact the reputation and need to be managed simultaneously. It is therefore important that everyone in the organisation understands and works towards optimal reputation management.

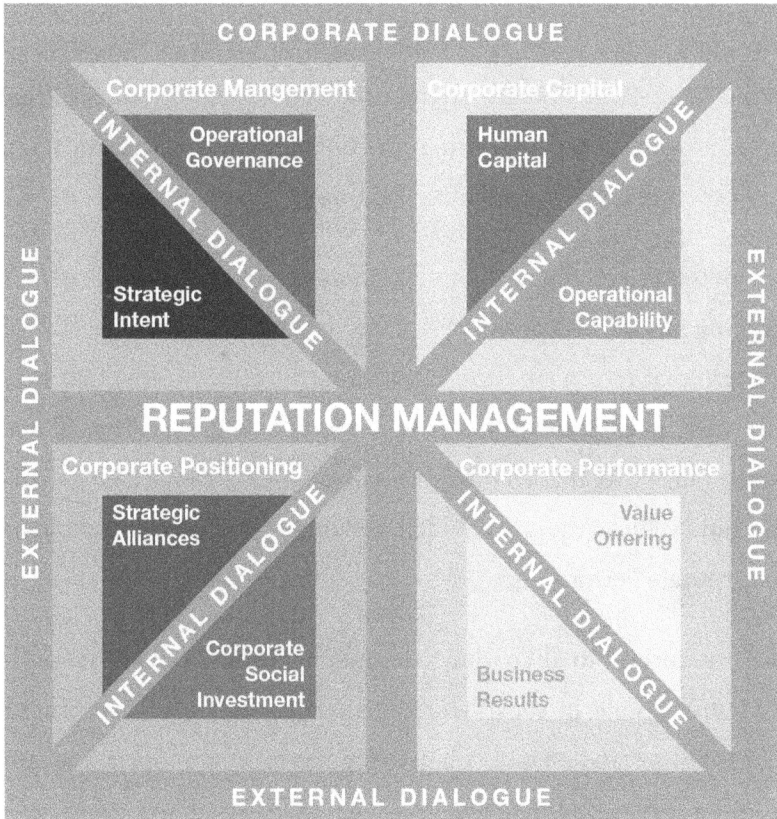

First things first, you need to know where the business is heading, what it wants to achieve and who will be leading the team to achieve the results. Then it is important to know how this will be achieved; what are the processes, policies and procedures to be followed? (Corporate Management).

Once this is in place, you need to make sure that you have the right team, armed with the right and most effective tools, on your side to achieve this vision (Corporate Capital). Then it will be of benefit to you to have a look at your partners, suppliers and other associated connections to your organisation and determine whether you share the same core values. Also have a look at your CSI initiatives to make sure that they are aligned to your organisation's strategic intent and that you are making a sustainable and positive impact in the community (Corporate Positioning).

From there, interrogate your value offering and make sure that your pricing model meets or, at best, exceeds the customers' expectation in terms of return on their investment. In other words, that they see value in their investment in the products and services that you offer. Make sure that your business dealings are transparent, ethical and add value to the shareholders and other associated stakeholders (Corporate Performance).

It is important to align your communication initiatives internally to boost morale, be sensitive about changes that happen within the organisation and ensure you're using the most appropriate means to get a message across.

Once your house is in order, you can engage with the outside world, ideally with an integrated communication strategy and plan to reach out and engage with the most appropriate stakeholder groups, using relevant channels of communication and encouraging feedback. This means a two-way conversation, and taking feedback and suggestions received from stakeholders to heart.

STRATEGIC INTENT Things to take into consideration when it comes to **strategic intent** and your reputation:

» Don't underestimate the value of having a clear vision and mission statement in place.

» Clearly define your vision and mission; and communicate this regularly.

» Don't assume that your stakeholders, especially your employees, know what the organisation's vision is.

» Align all your communication initiatives to your organisation's vision so that all stakeholders are on the same page and know what it is that they are working towards and what it is that they are supporting.

» Have two-way communication channels in place so that you can check that the messages you send out are indeed being interpreted correctly.

» As a leader you need to step out of your operational role and strategically see where the department, division, branch or company is heading.

» A good leader outlines the future state of the business beyond their own tenure, putting building blocks for a sustainable organisation in place for their successors.

» The CEO and the senior team must communicate the vision throughout the organisation and act decisively and collectively to meet expectations.

» The corporate brand of an organisation is infused with the personal attributes of its leaders – the more senior the executive, the closer the fit between the corporate and personal brands.

» Intelligent organisations make perception management part of their senior executive training regimen.

» Managerial and leadership skills development courses are critical to get leaders and managers to work on the business rather than in the business, and to get their teams to implement the strategy.

? Questions to ask yourself and your stakeholders

1. Do we have a clear vision and mission and do all our stakeholders, especially our employees know what it is?

2. Will the next person who walks into my office know what our company's vision is?

3. Do we have a communication management department, or at minimum someone that manages our communication?

4. Do we have a communication strategy

5. Do all the leaders in the organisation lead by example?

6. When last did I attend a leadership course?

7. How operationally involved are our managers/leaders?

8. Have all the managers on the team attended leadership training?

9. Does perception/reputation management form part of our senior management training?

10. When last did I communicate the future state of the business and beyond to the team?

CORPORATE GOVERNANCE Things to keep in mind when it comes to **corporate governance** and your reputation:

» Corporate governance refers to your company's rules, processes, procedures and policies. Operational governance essentially establishes the ground rules for conducting your day-to-day business; it is about agreeing on what needs to be done, how it should be done and by whom.

» A consistently positive stakeholder experience builds reliability, which builds trust and ultimately establishes a strong reputation.

» Whether you are being unfailingly consistent or consistently unpredictable, you are in the process of building a reputation for yourself.

» How ethical you are and what your business practices are, play an important role in how you govern the work you do.

» Every organisation needs to define their own key stakeholder groups, each with its own set of governing structures and communication platforms. When everyone speaks the same language, it eliminates confusion and inconsistency and ultimately builds trust in how the company operates.

» Your personal and business ethics have to be unfailing when running a business – this will have a direct impact on your organisation's reputation.

» The way that you act when no one is around is what makes up your moral fibre. It is important that your personal and business values be aligned and reflected in all areas of your life.

» Reputation and integrity are more than just buzzwords to be used in PR and marketing campaigns.

» The price of a good corporate reputation is eternal vigilance.

» However tempting it is in the short run to conceal unpleasant truths, falsehoods lead to distrust in the relationship and ruins reputations.

» Make sure that you ethically comply with regulations such as B-BBEE.

? Questions to ask yourself and your stakeholders

1. Are our policies and procedures clear and accessible to everyone internally?

2. Is the level of service or the products that we offer consistently of the same high standard and quality?

3. Is the service received from the newest person on the team the same as someone who has been on the team the longest?

4. How often do we check and update our procedures?

5. Do the ethics and core values of our team, partners and associated stakeholders resonate with ours/that of the business?

6. Are my personal and business values aligned?

7. Do I know who our stakeholders are? If so, do they each have clearly defined governance structures and communication platforms?

8. What structures do we have in place to monitor our reputation?

9. Do we have a communication process in place to have open channels of communication especially when there are unpleasant topics that need to be divulged?

10. Do we ethically comply with B-BBEE regulations?

HUMAN CAPITAL Things to keep in mind when it comes to **human capital** and your reputation:

» Your employees are a reflection and extension of you, select them carefully

» Have a comprehensive recruitment process in place.

» Have your ear to the ground and listen to what your employees are saying and keep an eye on what they are doing

» Build reputation management into the induction process.

» Build a culture of dissatisfaction so that you and your team continually strive for greater improvement.

? **Questions to ask yourself and your stakeholders**

1. Do we know what calibre recruit we need on the team?

2. Do we have a comprehensive recruitment process in place?

3. What does our induction process look like?

4. Is reputation management built into the induction session?

5. Do I have a close relationship with my team?

6. When last did I touch base with my team?

7. Does my team regard me as a mentor?

8. Are there internal channels of communication in place for my team to give me feedback?

9. What processes do we have in place to use feedback received from the team to continuously improve our service/product delivery?

10. Do I take the feedback received from the team to heart and act on it?

OPERATIONAL CAPITAL Things to keep in mind when it comes to **operational capital** and your reputation

» Arm your employees with the most appropriate and effective tools

» Keep it simple – you can do amazing things with inexpensive technology ideas.

» Align your business' technology needs to your overall business strategy.

» Let your technology choices be kind to the environment.

» Don't fall for the latest fads.

» Consider your technology partners carefully.

» Continuously look for ways to improve your project and/or service offering

» Nurture your IP and let your audiences know about it

» Be inventive and effective at solving client problems, this will lay a foundation for best practice

? Questions to ask yourself and your stakeholders

1. Does my team have the most appropriate tools to …?

2. Have we invested in the most effectives tools for the team to …?

3. Do we offer mentoring and continuous training for our team?

4. Are the tools that we using helping us to achieve our overall business strategy?

5. Do we take the environment into consideration when investing in tools, or are we driven by economic choices?

6. Do we have a process in place to select suppliers?

7. Do suppliers resonate with our values?

8. How do we manage and protect our IP?

9. Are our customers aware of our amazing IP?

10. Do we know what the industry best practises are?

STRATEGIC ALLIANCES Things to keep in mind when it comes to **strategic alliances** and your reputation

» Make sure that all the stakeholders you align yourself with have the same core values as you and your organisation.

» Choose your partners, affiliates and sponsors carefully.

» Do business with family and friends at your own risk.

» Know with whom you want to do business.

» Understand the environment in which you operate.

» Build professional friends.

» Retain the clients you have – it is more costly to find new clients.

» Be consistent when building relationships and fostering client relationships.

? Questions to ask yourself and your stakeholders

1. Do all the stakeholders that we are aligned and associated with share our core values?

2. Do we have a process in place to select partners, sponsors and affiliates?

3. Is hiring [insert family member/friend's name] the best decision for our business and achieving our business objective?

4. Do I value a business relationship or friendship with [insert family member/friend's name] more?

5. Do we have a process in place to build, foster and maintain professional friendships when building a relationship with customers?

6. Do have a strategy in place to build a solid relationship with our current clients?

7. Has the management strategy regarding client relationship been communicated throughout the organisation?

8. Do we foster the relationship with all our stakeholders equally?

9. Do we pay our suppliers on time?

10. Are our customers raving fans?

CSI

Things to keep in mind when it comes to **CSI** and your reputation

»   Align your social investment projects to your strategic intent.

»   See how your daily business operations could link to a community upliftment project.

»   Involve your employees in your CSI decisions and projects.

»   If there is a media opportunity for the CSI project that you are involved in, make sure that the project is the focus, not your goodwill.

»   Use organisations such as Rotary to maximise your CSI budget to make a sustainable difference.

? Questions to ask yourself and your stakeholders

1. Do we have a CSI budget?

2. Do we have a CSI strategy in place?

3. Does my team know what our CSI initiatives are?

4. Have we included the employees in helping us identify possible upliftment projects?

5. Are the CSI projects that we get involved with making a sustainable difference?

6. Do our operations contribute positively to the community in which we operate?

7. If not, how can we link our daily business operations to a community upliftment project?

8. Are we doing a specific project just to get media coverage?

9. Have I investigated and explored how organisations such as Rotary can be used to help us maximise our CSI budget

10. Do our stakeholders know about the projects that we are involved with and encouraged to participate in them?

VALUE OFFERING Things to keep in mind when it comes to **value offering** and your reputation:

»   Make sure that you have sufficient cash flow and can invest back into product/service development.

»   Have a process in place to ensure payment for products and services.

»   Have a pricing process in place and communicate the associated value so that you don't undersell yourself, and that clients still see value in your product/ service

»   Invest in communicating the value offering and what the benefits and return on investment are when they select your products or services.

»   Continual innovation is important in addressing client needs and will enhance client belief in your products. If clients are familiar with your organisation and have a high regard for your products and services, they will be more likely to invest in your products and services than those of the competition.

» Steer away from giving your products and service away at no cost. This is the quickest way to diminish their value.

? Questions to ask yourself and your stakeholders

1. What does our company's cash flow look like at this moment? Cash-No or Cash Glow?

2. Do we have sufficient structures in place to follow-up on debtors and get paid timely?

3. Have all your our outstanding invoices due been paid?

4. Do clients understand our payment schedules and terms?

5. Does the team know what the invoicing and follow-up processes are?

6. Do we charge interest for late payments?

7. Do we have a pricing process in place that is communicated with the associated value so that we don't undersell ourselves?

8. Do customers understand what value and associated benefits they get when they select our service/products?

9. Are we continuously improving our service/product offering to enhance the clients' experiences, which will also get them to invest in additional/new services that we offer?

10. Are we giving any of our services/products away at no charge?

BUSINESS RESULTS Things to keep in mind when it comes to **business results** and your reputation:

» Be transparent in all your dealings, especially financial ones.

» Ethical behaviour is non-negotiable on all levels of the business.

» Continuously build value for your shareholders.

» Shareholder value is maximised by delighting clients and motivating employees.

» Pricing is an important element to generating income

» Reputation management is not only dependent on financial results and profitability; there needs to balance in all business operations.

? Questions to ask yourself and your stakeholders

1. Do I understand what is going on in the books?

2. How transparent are we in all our financial dealing?

3. How are we making sure that our financial dealings are ethical?

4. Do we have structures and disciplinary codes in place for non-compliance to ethical behaviour?

5. What are we doing to keep the shareholders happy?

6. Are we creating shareholder value by delighting clients and motivating employees?

7. Does our pricing structure generate sufficient profit?

8. Do I have a budget in place?

9. How regularly do I work on and refine the budget and pricing schedule?

10. Am I purely focussed on sales and profitability, or do I regard the other elements of the business important as well?

INTERNAL DIALOGUE Things to keep in mind when it comes to **internal dialogue** and your reputation

» Employees like to have a voice and to be heard. Facilitate feedback opportunities through different forums.

» Be careful not to follow blanket stereotypes when communicating to different generations[1]. However, take into account that different generations have preferred working and learning requirements. This includes meetings and recognition programmes.

» Expand your communication strategies. Most companies rely too heavily on one strategy for corporate communication. By making the same message available in multiple formats, you'll ensure that you reach all employees.

» Make mentoring a constant. As your more established and experienced employees head toward retirement, develop strategies to ensure knowledge transfer and capture of organisational memory.

---

1   Wall Street Journal How-To Guides, *loc. cit.*

» Leaders must remain open to new ideas and provide constant feedback, working with managers and staff to shape the company's strategic vision. They must avoid projecting their own expectations about work and remain open to different perspectives based on generational attitudes.[2]

» When it comes to change management remember to:

› Have a change vision.

› Identify all the stakeholders that you need to communicate the change to.

› Have top level buy-in and visibly seeing embracing the change.

› Identify change agents.

› Have a comprehensive communication strategy and plan to support the change. Highlight how people will be impacted, what is required from them, and what training and support to provide.

› Keep in mind that you are dealing with people who are emotional beings and take their state of mind into consideration.

---

2   American Management Association, *loc. cit.*

? Questions to ask yourself and your stakeholders

1. Do we have regular communication with our employees?

2. Do we use different channels of communication to engage with our teams?

3. Are the channels of communication that we use relevant for them?

4. Do we have internal channels of communication/forums encouraging employee feedback?

5. Do we have mentorship support for new team members?

6. Do we act on the feedback given to us?

7. How many different generations do we have on the team?

8. Do I understand how best to communicate to each of the different generations?

9. Do I or the leader of the organisation, have a regular voice internally and is it my/their opinions that are communicated?

10. Do I know what steps to take should there be a change in the organisation that needs to be managed?

EXTERNAL DIALOGUE Things to keep in mind when it comes to **external dialogue** and your reputation

» Invest in research and understand what is important to your stakeholders and how you measure up. This will provide you with valuable insights and help you to align your communication initiatives accordingly.

» The entire internal organisation has an impact on how it is seen externally.

» Know who your stakeholders are, refine your message(s) for each group and use the most appropriate channels of communication.

» Remember that it is about storytelling and not just about regurgitating the key messages

» Have feedback mechanisms in place.

» Invest in media training for the whole team.

» There is no such thing as 'no comment' or 'off the record'. Remember to give your company's contact details during an interview, when possible, and remember to include a human element, i.e. a story

» Have an integrated communication strategy in place, i.e. use a mixture of traditional media (editorials), advertising and social media.

» Align your corporate image to your strategic intent. Test and measure it to see if your stakeholders resonate with it.

» Align all your marketing collateral to have the same look and feel, invest in a 'brand Bible' to align your organisation's brand

» Don't have a social media page just for the sake of it – if you do, steer away from the temptation of getting a newly appointed intern to manage it.

? Questions to ask yourself and your stakeholders

1. How are we keeping track of our organisation's reputation?

2. Have we ever conducted reputation management research? How did we measure up?

3. Do we have a comprehensive understanding of who our stakeholders are, what to communicate to them, and how best to get the message across?

4. Do I know what our company's communication strategy and plan is?

5. What feedback channels of communication do we have in place?

6. Have I and the executive team, attended media training in the last 12 months?

7. If a camera crew from an investigative television program were to knock on our doors and demand an interview, would I know how best to handle the situation?

8. Do we have a guideline in place to know how to use our company's logo?

9. Do we have a social media presence?

10. Who is currently managing our social media pages?

BIBLIOGRAPHY

Adendorff, S.A. & De Wit, P.W.C. 1997. *Production and operations management – a South African perspective*. 2nd ed. Thomson Publishing: Johannesburg.

American Management Association. 2014. *Leading the Four Generations at Work*. http://www.amanet.org/training/articles/Leading-the-Four-Generations-at-Work.aspx. Viewed 29/10/2015

Anon. 2001. What Drives Employee Satisfaction? *Community Banker*, 10(7):42-43

Anon. 2002. Employee Loyalty: It's Still There, But It's Different Now. *HR Focus*, 79(7):26.

Anon. 2003. BEE Moves to Centre Stage. *Southern Africa Monitor*, 8(3):1-4.

Antunovich, P., Laster, D. & Mitnick, S. 2000. Are high-quality firms also high-quality investments? *Current Issues in Economics and Finance*, 6(1):1-6.

Austin, D. 2002. Environmental Risks Could Reduce Shareholder Value of Oil and Gas Companies. *Energy User News*, 27(9):42.

Avlonitis, J. and Papastathopoulou, P. 2000. Marketing communications and product performance: innovative vs. non-innovative new retail financial products. *The International Journal of Bank Marketing*, 18(1):27-41.

Balmer, J.M.T. 2001. Corporate identity, corporate branding and corporate marketing – Seeing through the fog. *European Journal of Marketing*, 35(3/4): 248-291.

Balmer, J.M.T. and Gray, E.R. 1999. Corporate identity and corporate communications: creating a competitive advantage. *Corporate communications: An International Journal*, 4(4):171-177.

Bennett, R. and Kottasz, R. 2000. Practitioner perceptions of corporate reputation: an empirical investigation. *Corporate communications*, 5(4):224-234.

Bennett, R. and Gabriel, H. 2001. Reputation, trust and supplier commitment: The case of shipping organisation/seaport relations. *The Journal of Business & Industrial Marketing*,16(6/7): 424-438.

Berman, B. and Woods, J.D. 2002. Positioning IP for shareholder value. *Managing Intellectual Property*, 117:41–47.

Bernstel, J.B. 2003. Inner Branding. *Bank Marketing*, 35(3):14-19.

Bickerton, D. 2000. Corporate reputation versus corporate branding: the realist debate. *Corporate communications*, 5(1):42– 8.

Booker, E. 2002. Valuing the corporate brand in a downtown. *B to B*, 87(6):8.

Bowen, J.T. and Chen, S. 2001. The relationship between customer loyalty and customer satisfaction. *International Journal of Contemporary Hospitality Management*, 13(5):213-217.

Bown, A. 2015. *Comparing Apples and Oranges?* Charisma Communications. http://www.ngopulse.org/article/csi-or-csr-are-you-learning-npo. Viewed 29/10/2015.

Bromley, D. 2002. Comparing corporate reputations: League tables, quotients, benchmarks, or case studies? *Corporate Reputation Review*, 5(1):35-50.

Business Dictionary. 2015. *Change management*. http://www. businessdictionary.com/definition/change-management. html#ixzz3lmXMhGYh. Viewed 29/10/2015.

CareerFAQs. 2014. *Workplace Warfare: Baby Boomers, Gen X and Gen Y.* http://www.careerfaqs.com.au/news/news-and-views/workplace-warfare-baby-boomers-gen-x-and-gen-y. Viewed 29/10/2015.

Christensen, L.T. 2002. Corporate communication: the challenge of transparency. Corporate communications: *An International Journal*, 7(3):162-168.

Christensen, L.T. and Askegaard, S. 2001. Corporate identity and corporate image revisited: A semiotic perspective. *European Journal of Marketing*, 35(3/4):292-31.

Connelly, M. 2015. *Change Management Coach: What is Change Management?* http://www.change-management-coach.com/what-is-change-management.html. Viewed 29/10/2015.

Covey S. R. 1989. *The 7 Habits of Highly Effective People*. New York: Free Press.

Davies, G., Chun, R., da Silva, R.V. & Roper, S. 2001. The personification metaphor as a measurement approach for corporate reputation. *Corporate Reputation*, 4(2):113-127.

Davis, S. 2002. Brand Asset Management: how businesses can profit from the power of brand. *Journal of Consumer Marketing*, 19(4)351-358.

Davis, S.M. and Dunn, M. 2002. *Building the brand driven business – operationalize your brand to drive profitable growth*. United States of America: Jossey-bass-a Wiley Imprint.

De Chernatony, L. 2002. Living the Corporate Brand: Brand Values and Brand Enactment. *Corporate Reputation Review*, 5(2/3):113-130.

Deloitte. 2014. *2014 global survey on reputation risk: Reputation@Risk*. www. deloitte.com/reputationrisksurvey. Viewed 29/10/2015.

Department of Trade and Industry. 2015. *Economic Empowerment*. https://www.thedti.gov.za/economic_empowerment/bee.jsp. Viewed 29/10/2015.

Edgett, S. and Snow, K. 1997. Benchmarking measures of customer satisfaction, quality and performance for new financial service products. *Journal of Product and Brand Management*, 6(4):250–259.

Einwiller, S. and Will, M. 2002. *Towards an integrated approach to corporate branding – an empirical study*. MCB University Press, 7(2):100–109.

Ettorre, B. 1996. The care and feeding of a corporate reputation. *Management Review*, 85(6):39-43.

Financial Times Lexicon. http://lexicon.ft.com/Term? Viewed 29/10/2015.

Fisher, J. 2002. Surface and deep approaches to business ethics. *Leadership & Organization Development Journal*, 24(2):96-101.

Frankental, P. 2001. Corporate social responsibility – a PR invention? *An International Journal*, 6(1):18-23.

Gary, E.R. and Smeltzer, L.R. 1985. SMR Forum: Corporate Image – An Integral Part of Strategy. *Sloan Management Review*, 26(4):73-79.

George, W.W. 2001. Medtronic's Chairman William George on how mission-driven companies create long-term shareholder value. *Academy of Management Executive*, 15(4):39.

Goldberg, A. I., Cohen, G. & Fiegenbaum, A. 2003. Reputation building: Small business strategies for successful venture development. *Journal of Small Business Management*, 41(2):168-186.

Gotsi, M. and Wilson, A. 2001. Corporate reputation management: "living the brand". *Management Decision*, 39(2):99-104.

Grulke, W with Silber,G. 2002. *Lessons in Radical Innovation*, Financial Series Prentice Hall, Essex.

Harris, F. and De Chernatony, L. 2001. Corporate branding and corporate brand performance. *European Journal of Marketing*, 35(3/4):441-456.

Howarth, A. 2002. Get started in corporate social responsibility. *Financial Management* (CIMA), (1):5.

Institute of Directors Sustainable Development Forum. 2013. *Position Paper 7: Finding Business Value in Social Sustainability*. http://c.ymcdn.com/ sites/www.iodsa.co.za/resource/collection/4B905E82-99EB-48B1-BCDA-

F63F37069065/SDF_Position_Paper_7_Finding_Business_Value_In_ Social_Sustainability.pdf. Viewed 29/10/2015.

Joyner, B.E., Payne, D. & Raiborn, C.A. 2002. Building Values, Business Ethics and Corporate Social Responsibility Into The Developing Organization. *Journal of Developmental Entrepreneurship*, 7(1):113–131.

Klein, P. 1999. Measure what matters. *Communication World*, 16(i9):32.

Kowalczyk, S.J. and Pawlish, M.J. 2002. Corporate branding through external perception of organizational culture. *Corporate Reputation Review*, 5(2/3)159-174.

Koys, D.J. 2001. The effects of employee satisfaction, organizational citizenship, behavior, and turnover on organizational effectiveness: a unit-level, longitudinal study. *Personnel Psychology*, 54(1):101-113.

Kübler-Ross, E. R. 1969. *On Death and Dying*. New York: The Macmillan Company.

Lam, K. 2003. Executive branding. *Executive Excellence Provo*, 20(2):13.

Lantos, G.P. 2002. The ethicality of altruistic corporate social responsibility. *Journal of Consumer Marketing*, 19(3):205-232.

Lars, G. 2001. Using employee satisfaction measurement to improve people management: An adaptation of Kano's quality types. *Total Quality Management*, 12(7):949-957.

LePla, F.J. and Parker, L.M. 2002. *Integrated branding – becoming brand-driven through organisation-wide action*. London: Biddles.

Lund, D.B. 2003. Organizational culture and job satisfaction. *The Journal of Business and Industrial Marketing*, 18(3):219-236.

Maignan, I. and Ralston, D.A. 2002. Corporate Social Responsibility in Europe and the U.S. Insights from Businesses' Self-presentations. *Journal of International Business Studies*, 33(3):497.

Mastal, M.L. 2001. Mirror, mirror. *Oil & Gas Investor*, 21(5):57-59.

Matthews, D.H. 2003. Environmental management systems for internal corporate environmental benchmarking. *Benchmarking: An International Journal*, 10(2):95-106.

May, G.L. and Kahnweiler, B. 2002. Shareholder value: Is there common ground? *Alexandria*, 56(7):44-52.

Mayo, C. 2002. Too many codes, too much box ticking, too little shareholder value? *Corporate Finance*, 215:2.

McEwen, W.J. and Fleming, J.H. 2003. Customer Satisfaction Doesn't Count. *Gallup Management Journal Online*, (1):1.

McNaughton, L. 2003. Sales and Marketing Insights: The Value of the Corporate Brand. *Chemical Market Reporter*, 263(6):13-15.

Miller, M. 2013. *Generational Communication Style*. https://careerpivot. com/2013/communication-style-generational-workplace. Viewed 29/10/2015.

Mitchell, A. 2002. Will the real shareholder value please stand out? *Marketing week*, 25(28):28-30.

Moir, L. 2001. What do we mean by corporate social responsibility? *Corporate Governance*, 1(2):16-22.

Morgan, G. and Takahashi, Y. 2002. Shareholder Value in the Japanese Context. *Competition & Change*, 6(2):169-191.

Nakra, P. 2000. Corporate Reputation Management: 'CRM' with a Strategic Twist? *Public Relations Quarterly*, 45(2):35-42.

Needleman, T. 2003. Customer Satisfaction Is Supreme. *Internet World*, 9(5):6-7.

Newman, K. 2001. Interrogating SERVQUAL: a critical assessment of service quality measurement in a high street retail bank. *The International Journal of Bank Marketing*,19(3):126-139.

O'Connor. N. 2001. UK corporate reputation management: The role of public relations planning, research and evaluation in a new framework of organisation reporting. *Journal of Communication Management*, 6(1):54-63.

Prosci Change Management Learning Center. 2007. *ADKAR: Change Management Model*. http://www.change-management.com/tutorial-adkar-overview.htm. Viewed 29/10/2015.

Public Relations Institute of Southern Africa. 2015. *Professional Public Relations Practice and your company.* www.prisa.co.za/about-us/ professional-public-relations-and-your-company. Viewed 29/10/2015.

Ross, S. 2002. Making the rewards fit the degree of customer loyalty. *New Media Age,* (1):19.

Rottenberg, L. 2014. *Crazy is a Compliment: The Power of Zigging when Everyone Else Zags.* Penguin, New York.

Sarkis, J. 2003. Corporate environmental benchmarking. *Benchmarking: An International Journal,* 10(2):1.

Schiebel, W. and Pöchtrager, S. 2003. Corporate ethics as a factor for success – the measurement instrument of the University of Agricultural Sciences (BOKU), Vienna. *Supply Chain Management – An International Journal,* 8(2):116-121.

Schilling, R. 2003. Customer-Satisfaction Confidential. *American Drycleaner,* 69(12):30-33.

Schultz, M. and De Chernatony, L. 2002. Introduction: The challenges of corporate branding. *Corporate Reputation Review,* 5(2/3):105-112.

Schultz, V. and Buys, A. 2011. *Dependency to Dignity.* A2B Entrepreneurial Movement: Pretoria, South Africa.

Schwartz, P. 2000. When good companies do bad things. *Strategy and Leadership,* 28(3):4-11.

Silvestro, R. 2002. Dispelling the modern myth: Employee satisfaction and loyalty drive service profitability. *International Journal of Operations & Production Management,* 22(1):30-49.

Smith, K. 2002. ISO Considers Corporate Social Responsibility Standards. *Journal for Quality & Participation,* 25(3):42.

Sobol, M.G., Farrelly, G.E. & Taper, J.S. 1992. *Shaping the Corporate Image – An analytic guide for executive decision-makers.* Quorum Books: New York.

Solheim, N. 2012. *How to communicate with baby boomers.* http://www. benefitspro.com/2012/07/10/how-to-communicate-with-baby-boomers. Viewed 29/10/2015.

Steyn. B, and Puth, G. 2000. *Corporate Communication Strategy.* Heinemann: Sandown.

Taina, R. 2002. Team-building leads to increased productivity, employee satisfaction. *Caribbean Business,* 30(24):22.

Tallman, S. and Fladmoe-Lindquist, K. 2002. Internationalization, Globalization, and Capability-Based Strategy. *California Management Review,* 45(1):116-135.

Testa, M. R. 2002. A model for organisation-based 360 degree leadership assessment. *Leadership & Organisation Development Journal,* 23(5):260-268.

The Wall Street Journal How-To Guides: Managing your People. 2015. *How to Manage Different Generations.* http://guides.wsj.com/management/ managing-your-people/how-to-manage-different-generations. Viewed 29/10/2015.

Van der Walt, A., Strydom, J.W., Marx, S. & Jooste, C.J. 1996. *Marketing Management.* 3rd ed. Juta: Pretoria.

Van Heerden, C.H. and Puth, G. 1995. Factors that determine the corporate image of South African banking institutions an exploratory investigation. *International Journal of Bank Marketing,*13(3):12-17.

Weber Shandwick. 2015. *External CEO Engagement is Now a Mandate for Building Company Reputation.* http://www.themarketingsite.com/ news/39823/external-ceo-engagement-is-now-amandate-for-building-company-reputation. Viewed 29/10/2015.

Weldon, S. 2003. Communicating corporate social responsibility at Go-Ahead. *Strategic Communication Management,* 7(30):4.

Wilson, R. 2003. Keeping a watch on corporate reputation. *Strategic Communication Management,* 7(1):16-19.

Zairi, M. 2000. Social responsibility and impact on society. *The TQM Magazine,* 12(3):172-178.

Zyglidopoulos, S.C. 2001. The impact of accidents on firms' reputation for social performance. *Business and Society,* 40(4):416-441.

ABOUT THE AUTHOR

Regine is a corporate reputation specialist. She completed her Communication Management Honours degree Cum Laude at the University of Pretoria in 2001, and completed her MCom within a year.

Regine founded Reputation Matters in 2005 and hand picks and manages several teams that implement communication strategies.

She has gained much practical experience through several Communication, Change and Marketing Strategies compiled for clients in both the private and public domains. Regine developed the Repudometer®, which is one of the first tools that has been developed to measure organisational reputation.

Regine was the 2015/2016 Chairperson for the Western Cape Public Relations Institute of Southern Africa (PRISA) Committee, and was on the Board of the Rotary Club of Newlands, responsible for Public Image, and also chaired Rotary International's Public Image for District 9350.

Over weekends you will find her donning her pink skort for the Hout Bay Harriers.

www.ingramcontent.com/pod-product-compliance
Lightning Source LLC
Chambersburg PA
CBHW072307210326
41519CB00057B/3052